A Prophet for Today

Contemporary Lessons from the Book of Yehoshua

Rabbi Steven Pruzansky

Jerusalem • New York

Copyright © Rabbi Steven Pruzansky
Jerusalem 2006 / 5766

All rights reserved. No part of this publication may be translated, reproduced, stored in a retrieval system or transmitted, in any form or by any means, electronic, mechanical, photocopying, recording or otherwise, without express written permission from the Author.

Typesetting: Jerusalem Typesetting, Jerusalem
Cover Design: S. Kim Glassman

ISBN 9789652293558

1 3 5 7 9 8 6 4 2

Gefen Publishing House
6 Hatzvi Street, Jerusalem 94386, Israel
972-2-538-0247 • orders@gefenpublishing.com

Gefen Books
600 Broadway, Lynbrook, NY 11563, USA
1-800-477-5257 • orders@gefenpublishing.com

www.israelbooks.com

Printed in Israel

Send for our free catalogue

This book is dedicated by

יעקב and לאה פיגה
Berkowitz

In honor of our children
איתן מאיר בן יעקב יהושע
יונתן אפרים בן יעקב יהושע
פנחס זכרי״ה בן יעקב יהושע
Berkowitz

In honor of our parents

משה דוד בן שרגא פייבעל
אסתר ליבע בת הרב אפרים מיכל הלוי
Berkowitz

משה אריה בן אברהם יצחק
רבקה בת פינחס
Beer

לזכר נשמות
הרב אפרים מיכל בן זאב נחמי״ה הלוי
פעשע ביילע בת הרב אהרן אשר
הרב ישראל יהודה בן הרב אפרים מיכל הלוי
Pruzansky

שרגא פייבל בן יעקב
מאשא בת זכריה לב
Berkowitz

אברהם יצחק בן יונה
חנה בילה בת מנחם מנדל הלוי
Beer

פנחס בן דוד אייזיק
רייזל בת משה
Slodzin

הרב דוב בערל וויין
שדרות בן מימון 15, ירושלים 92262

בס"ד ג' אדר תשנ"ו

Dear Rabbi Steven — שיחי'

I have reviewed the manuscript on ספר יונה that you have sent me. It is really an excellent piece of work and scholarship. The danger in it and the criticism that you will undoubtedly receive is in your attempt to fit events and insights from the ספר יונה to present-day Israeli scene. Many of the leading rabbis of our time have warned against attempting such comparisons. However, this is not a unanimous opinion for otherwise what is the purpose of studying תנ"ך. I definitely think the book should be published and distributed. It is very well written and contains excellent insights. I wish you great success with it.

Best regards and all blessings,

בברכת התורה

הרב דוב בערל וויין
ירושלים

בס"ד

כ"ח תשרי תשס"ה

I have reviewed the manuscript on ספר יהושע that you have sent me. It is really an excellent piece of work and scholarship.

The danger in it and the criticism that you will undoubtedly receive is in your attempt to fit events and insights from the ספר יהושע to the present-day Israeli scene. Many of the leading Rabbis of our time have warned against attempting such comparisons.

However, this is not a unanimous opinion for otherwise what is the purpose of studying תנ"ך. I definitely think the book should be published and distributed. It is very well written and contains excellent insights.

I wish you great success with it.

Best regards and blessings,
בידידות והוקרה

Berel Wein

בס"ד

ישיבת רבינו יצחק אלחנן
ישיבה יוניברסיטי בישראל ע"ר
Yeshiva University in Israel
Gruss Kollel - Aaron Rakeffet
Caroline and Joseph S. Gruss Institute
POB 16095 Jerusalem 91160 ISRAEL Tel: 972-2-643-0326 Fax: 642-2659

My student Rabbi Steven Rozansky has written a profound manuscript on the Biblical volume of Yehoshua. He analyzes eight basic concepts in Yehoshua in accordance with classic commentaries and modern expositors. Rabbi Rozansky then elaborates on contemporary Israeli quests and challenges in the light of his understanding of Yehoshua.

This work should be read, studied and pondered by all those who recognize the inherent miracle of the reborn State of Israel. It will grant them insight and confidence in their attempts to influence the public gestalt of God and man. State of Israel before

I highly recommend <u>A Prophet for Today</u> to my colleagues, friends and students.

Aaron Rakeffet

20.IX.04 - כ׳ תשרי

ישיבת רבינו יצחק אלחנן
ישיבה יוניברסיטי בישראל ע"ר

GRUSS KOLLEL – AARON RAKEFFET

Caroline and Joseph S. Gruss Institute
POB 16095 Jerusalem 91160 ISRAEL · Tel: 972-2643-0326 Fax: 642-2659

My student, Rabbi Steven Pruzansky, has written a profound manuscript on the biblical volume of Yehoshua. He analyzes nine basic concepts in Yehoshua in accordance with classic commentaries and modern expositors. Rabbi Pruzansky then elaborates on contemporary Israeli quests and challenges in the light of his understanding of Yehoshua.

This work should be read, studied and pondered by all those who recognize the inherent miracle of the reborn state of Israel. It will grant them insight and confidence in their attempts to influence the public gestalt of the State of Israel before God and man.

I highly recommend "A Prophet for Today" to my colleagues, friends and students.

Aaron Rakeffet
20.IX.04 – ה' תשרי תשס"ה

*To my wife Karen,
my partner in life and love*

～ Acknowledgments

THIS BOOK is based on a series of lectures given at Congregation Bnai Yeshurun of Teaneck, New Jersey, where I have been privileged to serve as Rabbi since 1994. Many of the concepts and conclusions contained herein arose in response to questions and comments made by participants in these classes, to whom I am greatly indebted. I consider it a blessing to lead a congregation that is not only renowned for its kindness and generosity, but also for the fertile and creative intellectual environment that it promotes.

A traditional methodology, rather than a scientific or literary one, was employed in this study. I fully subscribe to the Rambam's fifth fundamental principle of Judaism that God communicates with man through prophecy, and therefore I approached the words of the prophets – including Yehoshua – with reverence and a yearning to reveal their deeper truths and messages. The classical sources – Talmud, Midrashim, Rashi, Radak, the Metzudot, Ralbag, Don Yitzchak Abarbanel and the Malbim – were all utilized, along with two contemporary commentaries: the work *Me-avoor Ha'aretz* (published privately in 1995), by Rav Avraham Remer, written from what can be loosely termed a "Religious-Zionist" perspective, and *Mishbetzot Zahav* (published privately in 2001), by Rav Shabtai Weiss, a compilation that reflects what can be loosely termed a "Yeshivish" perspective. All these commentaries ensure that *Navi* is not construed as merely a book, but as an integral part of the Torah and God's enduring message to mankind.

I want to thank Ilan Greenfield, the publisher of Gefen Publishing House, for his continued commitment to producing quality Jewish literature for the educated public; Projects Coordinator Smadar Belilty for her professionalism and diligence; and my editor Kezia Raffel Pride, for her professionalism, smooth prose and cogent insights.

I want to thank Rena and Mark Sokolow, for their technical assistance, inspiration and – most of all – their cherished friendship.

I would be greatly remiss if I did not acknowledge the two primary rabbinic influences in my life: the Rav of my youth, Rav Berel Wein, today of Yerushalayim, and my primary teacher, Rav Yisrael Chait, the Rosh Yeshiva of Yeshiva Bnei Torah in Far Rockaway, New York. Their thoughts inform almost every page of this book, although the contents are my responsibility alone. Both imbued in me a love of Torah.

That love of Torah was nurtured by my parents, Sylvia and Wallace Pruzansky, who have been constant sources of support and encouragement for my entire life, and my in-laws, Suzanne and Oscar Hausdorff, whose thoughtfulness and passion for dialogue, have, over many years, obliged me to crystallize and defend my ideas in many realms. I also benefited tremendously in Torah and *midot* from my grandparents, of blessed memory: Pesha and Rav Ephraim Pruzansky of the Bronx, New York (whose classes in *Navi* at the Young Israel of Pelham Parkway prove, I suppose, that the apple does not fall far from the tree) and Lillian and Hyman Schneider of Netanya, Israel (for whom a *shul* was always a second home). Not a day goes by during which I do not think of them and the high standards they maintained of observance of *mitzvot*, love of Torah and pursuit of goodness. May their memory continue to be a blessing for our entire family.

My children are a constant source of joy, and my love for them is boundless. To Ayelet and Shmuly Katz, Tamar and Ari Ginsberg, Dina Pruzansky and Ari Pruzansky, nothing pleases me more than to be known as your father. And my young grandchildren, Yona Leah Katz and Ari Katz, bring immeasurable delight to my life. They all have a primary share in this book.

Finally, my dear wife Karen – to whom this book is dedicated – did more than urge me to write. She encouraged me many years ago, probably against her better judgment, to leave the practice of law and enter the rabbinate. No one is as selfless, as caring, as sensitive and as loving. Sharing my life with her has brought me untold rewards that simple words cannot fully express. To her I owe my deepest gratitude and appreciation. May *Hashem* continue to shower His blessings upon her, our children and grandchildren, our parents and extended family of brothers and sisters, and nieces and nephews.

I conclude with a prayer that, in these difficult times of disengagement and forced withdrawal from the land of Israel – when the point of contention between the two camps in Jewish life is the philosophical approach to the land of Israel – the Book of Yehoshua provide us with a basis for thought, dialogue, guidance and perhaps even inspiration in the years ahead.

Steven Pruzansky
Teaneck, New Jersey, *Tevet 5766 – January 2006*

Contents

Introduction:		xv
Chapter One:	The Spies and Rachav	1
Chapter Two:	Crossing the Jordan	17
Chapter Three:	Yehoshua and the Angel of God	33
Chapter Four:	Conquest of Yericho	41
Chapter Five:	The First Sin: The Spoils of Achan	53
Chapter Six:	The Treaty with Givon	73
Chapter Seven:	Miracle at Givon	93
Chapter Eight:	Yehoshua and Calev	107
Chapter Nine:	The Division of the Land	121
Epilogue:		137
About the Author:		140

The Land of Israel
in the time of Yehoshua

LEBANON

Kinneret

Mediterranean Sea

Jordan River

Shechem
Shiloh
Bet-El • Ai
Givon
Ayalon • Yericho
Gilgal
Yerushalayim

Hevron

Dead Sea

TRANSJORDAN

SINAI

⁓ Introduction

THE TALMUD (Megila 14a) states: "The Jewish people had many prophets, twice the number of Jews who came out of Egypt. [So why are only the words of forty-eight prophets and seven prophetesses recorded?] Only the prophecy that was needed for future generations was written down, and that which was not needed for future generations was not written down."

The assertion that the study of Navi (Prophets) is neglected among the Jewish people will shock no one. Those who are fortunate are exposed to the words of the prophets in elementary and high school, where they are generally construed as "ancient Jewish history," the often-fascinating stories of the wars, kings, heroes, villains, transgressions and tragedies of the Jewish people. Beyond that, it is safe to assume that of the few Jews who encounter the words of the prophets at all, most do so only during the chanting of the weekly *haftara*, and strain to follow the words and attempt to discern a connection – conceptual, thematic or otherwise – between the *haftara* and the weekly Torah reading. We study the Talmud, immerse ourselves in *halacha* and review the *sedra* – and properly so – but a systematic, penetrating study of *Nach* is not on most people's learning agenda.

Occasionally, lectures on Navi will attempt to extract principles of *Musar* (ethical conduct) or serve as a peg on which to hang a discussion of *halacha* – all, again, extremely important and worthwhile. What is absent is a recognition that Navi has much to teach every generation and is especially relevant today, with events in the Jewish and general world unfolding at a dizzying pace. What is missing, ultimately, is an appreciation that "only the prophecy that was needed for future generations was written down," and therefore we are obligated to attempt to extract and derive those lessons from the words of our prophets.

One can easily see the contemporary applicability of the words of Yeshayahu or Yechezkel, or other prophets whose relatively few words are chronicled in the book of *Trei Asar*. Those prophets console and inspire, challenge and exhort, and their breadth of vision infuses our service of God with substance and hope. But what about other prophets, such as Yehoshua, popularly known as Joshua? We are not even accustomed to regarding Yehoshua as a prophet, but, indeed, he is cited right after Aharon in the *Seder Olam*'s list of the forty-eight prophets.[1] What does the Book of Yehoshua have to teach "all generations"? That is the subject of this work.

It is axiomatic that the Book of Yehoshua was given to us not merely as history but as prophecy, and must therefore lend itself to the same analysis as the other prophetic works. It must contain ideas that are essential to Jewish life through the ages. But Yehoshua has a second dimension that not only enhances its status as prophecy, but also makes it especially relevant to modern times. The Gemara (Nedarim 22b) states: "Rav Ada the son of Rabbi Chanina stated: 'If the Jewish people had not sinned, they only would have been given the Five Books of the Torah *and the Book of Yehoshua*, the latter because it teaches the disposition[2] (literally, the arrangement) of the land of Israel.'" The Book of Yehoshua is singled out as unique among the Prophets, as it outlined the allocation of the land of Israel to the tribes and thereby completed one of the essential themes of the Torah: the fulfillment of the divine promise of the land of Israel to our forefathers.

The phrase used by the Gemara – *erkah shel Eretz Yisrael* – can also be translated as "the value" or "worth" of the land of Israel. That is to say, most of the events of the Torah took place outside of the land of Israel, the Torah itself was given to us outside the land of Israel, and the Torah must be observed outside the land of Israel. Yehoshua – an entire book of *Tanach* – was dedicated to the conquest and division of the land of Israel to underscore that Israel is not tangential to our service of Hashem or our

---

1. See Rashi, Megila 14a.
2. The Hebrew word is *erkah,* which Rashi interprets as "the apportionment to each tribe of its share in the land."

observance of *mitzvot*, but is rather indispensable to a full and comprehensive Torah life. Our observance of *mitzvot* is limited outside the land, and, on one level, even construed as inferior. "Even after you are exiled, you should continue to be distinguished by the *mitzvot*. Continue to wear *tefillin*, affix *mezuzot* to your doorposts, etc., so that when you return to Israel, the commandments will not be new and unfamiliar to you."[3]

Ramban hastens to add that *mitzvot* are certainly incumbent upon Jews everywhere in the world, but there is a special dimension to their observance in the land of Israel.[4] Elsewhere, Ramban elaborates:

> The land of Israel, which is the center of civilization, is the heritage of God unique to His name… And so He sanctified the people who dwells on His land with the holiness of [the laws of forbidden] relations and the abundance of *mitzvot* for His name's sake… The land that is the heritage of His glorious name will expel its defilers and will not tolerate immorality or idolatry… As the Sifra states… "the land of Israel is not like other lands; it does not long suffer sinners."[5]

The land of Israel is intrinsically linked to Hashem, "whose eyes are always upon it from the beginning of the year to year's end" (Devarim 11:12).

As the Book of Yehoshua discusses the conquest and settlement of Israel, it is likely that its fundamental message contains lessons for our own national return to the land of Israel after a long and difficult sojourn in the exile – lessons relating to our mission, our destiny, our methods of conquest, our relations with our neighbors and among ourselves, and the means of securing Jewish possession of the land itself. These issues must be explored, understood, and applied. We cannot simply relegate Yehoshua to the dusty shelf of "ancient history" and say that there is nothing to learn from this *sefer*, because it was recorded "for all generations." Nor can we simply peruse the chapters and verses, and just attempt to imitate Yehoshua's mode of conquest or methodology. Yehoshua was guaranteed success and lived in a time in which the Jewish people still relied on God's open miracles, notwithstanding that the extent and swiftness of the conquest were dependent as well on the people's free choice and faithfulness to the Torah. Yehoshua's conquest was nevertheless a foregone conclusion.

3. Rashi, Devarim 11:18.
4. Ramban, Devarim 11:18.
5. Ramban, Vayikra 18:25.

We do not have that luxury – nothing is guaranteed in our world, except the ultimate coming of Moshiach, and so we cannot just try to ascertain what he did and duplicate it ourselves. Rather, we must derive lessons from each of the major events in the *sefer*, and attempt to apply them properly – to relate them to the trends and aspirations of the Jewish people today, and to the events through which we are living today. Certainly, there is much more that can be derived from the events in Yehoshua than what will be found here; this is merely a starting point, an attempt to look at Navi as not just a record of the past but as an intimation of the present and future.

Our modern return to the land of Israel has not been untroubled, to say the least. The successes were certainly beyond the wildest expectations of the Jewish world even one century ago. After nearly two millennia in exile, dispersed and victimized, the Jewish people arose and created a modern, relatively prosperous state, a homeland and gathering point for Jews around the world. Many, if not most, were motivated by the prophetic vision that foretold of an eventual return to the land after a brutal exile. There are more students of Torah today in Israel than ever before. But the failures – or the disappointments – have been striking. The secular Zionist dream of creating a state like all states so that Jews would again be a "normal" people, accepted in the world's tribunals, did not materialize. In most of the world, Israel is as scorned as the Jews in the exile ever were – if not more – and Jews remain pariahs despite our best efforts to achieve normalcy. The integration of Jews of different backgrounds has not gone particularly smoothly, and the primacy of the Torah as the spiritual and legal foundation of the state has never been accepted and remains a controversial topic. The very purposes of a Jewish state, and even the definition of "who is a Jew" vs. "who is an Israeli," have been the subject of vociferous debate without resolution.

There is nothing "normal" about the State of Israel – not its origins, not the ingathering of its Jewish citizens from across the globe, not the relentless and interminable hatred of its enemies, not its military triumphs against more numerous and powerful adversaries, not the world's intolerance of its elementary right of self-defense, not the constant discussions in the world's salons of its fundamental right to exist, and certainly not the mixture of the holy and the profane, the sacred and the secular, that has created two societies with little common ground between them.

The great issues of the day – security and peace, settlement or surrender, religion and state – are seemingly far from resolution, and the discussions are almost always informed – and can be predicted – by the individual's commitment (or lack of commitment) to Torah. For some in Israeli society, the successes of Israel have unleashed feelings of guilt and shame that are not easily assuaged, and have caused them to doubt the justice or morality of a Jewish state. The disappointments can almost all be attributed to a constricted vision of Jewish life and the role of a Jewish state in God's plan. For those who believe that our modern return to the land of Israel has – or can have – religious significance, the Book of Yehoshua has much to teach us – about the purposes of the land of Israel and the foundations of the Jewish state thereon.

The *Tanach* is divided into three parts (*Torah, Nevi'im* and *Ketuvim*, the Torah, the Prophets and the Writings). Jews maintain that the Torah is the literal word of Hashem, as dictated to Moshe in the wilderness of Sinai. Rambam[6] writes that the Ketuvim were written through *Ruach HaKodesh*, "divine inspiration," which, in terms of the forms of divine communication, is inferior to prophecy. But how can it be inferior, since some sections of the Prophets are duplicated in the Writings?[7] Rav Yosef Ber Soloveitchik, quoting his grandfather, Rav Chaim Soloveitchik, explained that the difference between Navi and Ketuvim is not in the level of divine inspiration, but something else: the words of the prophets were meant to be spoken, and only later to be written down. A *niv* – the root of the word *Navi* – is a message, in this context a communication from God that the prophet is obliged to deliver to God's people. Conversely, the Writings – as the term indicates – are words that are recorded – not uttered orally – and only after being written down are they read as well.[8]

This concept reinforces that the primary purpose of the "prophets of truth and righteousness"[9] was to convey God's word to the people, directly and orally. The *Sefer Yehoshua* was transcribed by Yehoshua himself.[10] If the words were therefore preserved for posterity, it is because there are lessons in it for today, and for all generations. That is the focus of our study,

---

6. Rambam, Moreh Nevuchim Part 2, Chapter 45.
7. For example, II Shmuel 22 and Tehillim 18.
8. *Chidushei HaGrach v'HaGriz al HaShas*, page 2. *Shiurei HaGrid*, page 28.
9. From the blessing preceding the *haftara*.
10. Bava Batra 14b.

to analyze the events that took place as we entered the land of Israel as a nation for the first time and thereby bring to life the words of the Book of Yehoshua.

For the Jews accompanying Yehoshua, four hundred and seventy years have elapsed since Hashem promised Avraham "to your descendants I have given this land"[11] and forty years since the Jewish people were liberated from Egypt by God's "great power and strong hand" (Shemot 32:11). The forty years in the wilderness were formative years, in which the Jewish people received and embraced the Torah, lived a miraculous existence, and stumbled not a few times on their march to the Promised Land. They are now ready to enter the land and fulfill their destiny: to be a "kingdom of priests and a holy nation" (Shemot 19:6), God's "beloved treasure among all the peoples" (Shemot 19:5), and His national representatives on earth. The tormented years of exile are behind them, and they are poised to begin the process of constructing the ideal Torah society as a model for the rest of mankind. The journey begins.

---

11. Breisheet 15:18; note the past tense of "I have given." The land is technically our possession already in Avraham's time. It only awaits our formal entry. See also Rashi's commentary to Shemot 12:40.

~(Chapter One
THE SPIES AND RACHAV

MOSHE'S DEATH concluded the final chapter of the written Torah, as well as a momentous era for the Jewish people. Moshe bid farewell to his people on the banks of the Jordan River. He would not enter the land of Israel, stripped of his authority and of life itself due to his failure of leadership at Meriva.[1] In his last official act, Moshe prophetically enunciated the unique traits of each of the tribes of Israel and what each was destined to contribute to the national welfare. He then departed this world at God's command.

At the beginning of the Book of Yehoshua, Yehoshua bin Nun, Moshe's faithful aide and disciple through forty years in the wilderness, assumed the leadership of Israel. He was understandably apprehensive. Any successor to a dominant, charismatic, and exalted figure such as Moshe would certainly pale by comparison. As impractical as it was for a longtime second-in-command to ever be perceived as leadership material, it was nearly impossible to envision anyone succeeding Moshe, whose personal greatness – and intimacy with God – exceeded that of any other human being. Yehoshua, as noble as he was, was no Moshe, a point that did not go unnoticed: "The elders of that generation said: 'Moshe's countenance is like the sun, and Yehoshua's countenance is like the moon. Woe for that shame, woe for that

---

1. Bamidbar 20:1–13.

disgrace.'"[2] Yehoshua's glory was not inherent but merely a reflection of Moshe's glory, and the generational decline was immediately apparent.[3]

Yehoshua's difficulties were exacerbated even more by the realization that these same people, who now longed for the great Moshe, had constantly harangued and tormented Moshe while he was alive. Moshe himself at one point – oddly enough, almost at the *beginning* of his tenure – cried out to God in frustration: "A bit more and they will stone me!" (Shemot 17:4). How much less tolerant would they be of Yehoshua, Moshe's underling, and his mission!

Moreover, it is human nature for people to yearn to breathe free and unwind after living under the rule of any overpowering leader, and certainly Moshe, the "man of God" (Devarim 33:1), whose very presence reminded them of God, Sinai, Torah, *mitzvot*, and the destiny of Israel. During his life, the Jews were ambivalent about Moshe,[4] and their feelings for Moshe colored their acceptance of Yehoshua.

At such a difficult political transition, a number of possibilities – a coup, a civil war, a schism – loom. To overcome Yehoshua's doubts, God appeared to him, confirmed his worthiness and his mission in the eyes of the people, and made two promises, one political and one spiritual: "No man will challenge you all the days of your life, and as I was with Moshe so shall I be with you. I will neither forsake you nor abandon you" (Yehoshua 1:5). Essentially, God informed Yehoshua firstly that he would face no overt political challenges or dissent during his career, and secondly that the divine presence would rest on Yehoshua as it did on Moshe. Yehoshua, too, would be the beneficiary of miracles as was Moshe.[5]

With that validation, and the dual charge of *chazak v'ematz*, "be strong and courageous" (Yehoshua 1:6–7) in leading the people and faithfully upholding the Torah, Yehoshua was commanded by God to cross the Jordan and begin the conquest of the land of Israel. He chose to do so, paradoxi-

---

2. Bava Batra 75a.
3. Rashi, Bava Batra 75a.
4. Rashi, Bamidbar 20:29 and Devarim 34:8. When Aharon died, *Vayivku... kol beit Yisrael*, the entire house of Israel cried over his loss, the men and the women. Whereas when Moshe died, *Vayivku Bnei Yisrael*, the Children of Israel – only the men – mourned his loss. Moshe, the lawgiver and disciplinarian, did not rate as highly in the people's estimation as did Aharon, the peacemaker.
5. Malbim.

cally enough, by duplicating one of his predecessor Moshe's *failures*, the mission of the spies.

> And Yehoshua bin Nun sent two men, spies, from the Shittim, discreetly saying, "go observe the land and Yericho," and they came to the house of a woman innkeeper named Rachav. (2:1)

Why was this mission necessary, especially since God had already told Yehoshua that he would successfully conquer the land? "For it is you who will cause this people to inherit the land that I swore to their fathers to give to them" (1:6). Certainly Yehoshua was in a prime position to realize the dangers of such a mission, having himself participated in the debacle of Moshe's spies, whose betrayal forced the Jewish people to spend forty years in the wilderness. Only the lives of Yehoshua and his colleague Calev ben Yefuneh were spared from that mission and, indeed, that entire generation. So, again on the verge of entering the land of Israel, why risk another disaster – especially since Yehoshua knew they would conquer the land through God's hand, in a miraculous way? The Jews were guaranteed that as long as they were faithful to the Torah, they would conquer Israel without even suffering any casualties. So why send spies at all?

Additionally, who were these unnamed men who apparently gave Yehoshua the confidence that they would not fail him? And what precisely did they uncover as a result of their reconnaissance? It seems as soon as they arrived at Rachav's inn, their presence was discovered, their identities were revealed, and their mission was jeopardized.

> The king of Yericho was told, "Behold, men have come here this night from the children of Israel to spy out the land." The king sent a message to Rachav, saying, "Bring out the men who have come to you, to your house, for they have come to spy out the land." (Yehoshua 2:2)

Unlike Moshe's spies who at least traversed the land, brought back its fruit and reported on the strengths and weaknesses of the inhabitants, Yehoshua's spies went immediately to Rachav, somewhat euphemistically described as an innkeeper. In reality, the phrase *isha zonah* means both innkeeper and harlot:[6] Rachav provided food and lodging to certain customers, and additional services to other clients. Her inn was therefore a local attraction, and surely a place where intelligence information could

---

6. Radak offers both as possibilities. Abravanel suggests that she was both.

be gathered easily. But why would these spies not simply reconnoiter the terrain and fortifications on their own – as tourists, perhaps – and then move on? Why would the holy conquest of the land of Israel – the fulfillment of God's covenant with our forefathers – be dependent on the good will of a prostitute? We must understand the background and personality of this interesting woman Rachav, who immediately defied her king and assisted the Jewish spies.

> The woman took the two men and hid them, and told the king: "It is true, men had come – from where, I do not know. But when the gates of the city were about to close at night, the men left, destination unknown. If you pursue them quickly, you will capture them." But she had hidden them on her roof, in the stalks of flax. (Yehoshua 2:4–6)

Rachav indicated that the spies had fled eastward, toward the Jordan River. This was logical, as Yericho was situated very close to the river, and surely the king knew that the Jews were encamped on the Jordan River's eastern bank. As the gates of the city closed behind the pursuers who would return empty-handed, Rachav approached her hidden visitors with words of inspiration.

> I know that God has given you the land, and that our people fear you, and the residents of the land have melted away because of you. We have heard how God dried up the waters of the Red Sea when you left Egypt, and what you did to the two kings of the Emori, Sichon and Og, who were across the Jordan, whom you completely destroyed. We heard, our hearts melted, and because of you our men were dispirited – because Your God is the God of the heavens above and the earth below. (Yehoshua 2:9–11)

What an insightful retrospective – historically and theologically – on the mission of Israel! As if she had been waiting for the opportunity to share these Torah thoughts, Rachav articulated in an instant what Moshe had attempted to inculcate in the Jewish people over forty years, and with only partial success. This is certainly impressive by the standards of any non-Jewish innkeeper; even more so for a brothel owner! From where did Rachav absorb this philosophy?

Before we analyze that, let us conclude with Rachav's request and the spies' response.

> Now swear to me by God that since I have been kind to you, you will be kind to my father's house, and give me a faithful sign that you will keep alive my father, my mother, my brothers, and my sisters, and all that is theirs, and you will save our souls from death. The men said to her: "We will die instead of you – if you do not relate this discussion of ours to others. Then, when God gives us this land, we will act towards you with kindness and truth." (Yehoshua 2:12–14)

Rachav asked that her family be saved, and the spies readily agreed in exchange for Rachav's agreement not to divulge their conversations about… what? What exactly did they learn from Rachav that aided their conquest of Israel? The text is silent about this. Yet, the three agreed on a sign that would ensure Rachav's protection. When the conquest of Yericho began, Rachav was to gather her entire family in her home, and hang a cord of scarlet thread from her window. That home and its inhabitants would be spared. What was the significance of that particular sign – the *chut hashani* – the scarlet thread?

In any event, Rachav helped them escape by lowering them on a rope from her window, which bordered on the city's outer wall – a good location for her business, apparently. The spies headed not east towards the Jordan and the camp of Israel, but west, towards the mountains, where they hid for three days until their return route was clear. When they returned to the camp of Israel, they reported their success, such as it was, to Yehoshua: "God has given the land into our hands, and all the inhabitants of the land have melted because of us" (2:24).

But what happened? What did they learn in these several days that they did not know before? What did Rachav contribute to the success of their impending conquest? Who was this Rachav?

Rachav

Clearly, Chazal understood Rachav's primary vocation as prostitution. The Gemara states (Megila 15a) that there were four extremely gorgeous women in history – Sarah, Rachav, Avigayil and Esther. Of the four, only Rachav was able to arouse a man simply by mention of her name. In her time, the very name Rachav possessed an intense eroticism that moved men into alluring worlds of fantasy and desire. To those who knew her and could visualize her, she was irresistible, and world-renowned – an international celebrity. And an excellent businesswoman.

"The wall of her house was the wall of the city's fortification" (2:15). The Midrash[7] comments that her local customers would enter her home city-side, through her front door, whereas travelers, brigands and others would come through her establishment's back entrance, located on the city wall.

How did Rachav know that "the men were dispirited" (2:11)? The Gemara (Zevachim 116a–b) relates this to male virility. As Israel's reputation grew and its army approached, the male Canaanite was afflicted with impotency brought on by fear of conquest. Rachav's business declined precipitously, and she was certainly in the best position to know the physical and psychological condition of the local combatants. "There was no minister or officer of the nations who did not have relations with Rachav."[8] She was world-class and world-famous, conducting her business throughout the forty years the Jewish people were in the wilderness.

And now? Note the power of *teshuva* (repentance)! "Let the cord of scarlet thread I used in my immoral business now be used for virtue." After she and her family were saved (6:25), Rachav converted to Judaism, at the age of fifty[9] married Yehoshua[10] himself (!) and became the ancestress of eight prophets who were also *kohanim*, including the prophetess Chulda and the prophet Yirmiyahu.[11] The Midrash[12] further extols Rachav as "one, like Yitro, who was brought near by God although she was not chosen by Him" (unlike Avraham, for example, who was chosen by God after initially drawing near on his own.) And the Yerushalmi[13] declares that "when the Jewish people follow God's will, God scours the entire world for righteous people that He can bring to cleave to His people, such as Yitro and Rachav…"[14] "Righteous" people? By what standard would Rachav be

---

7. *Sifrei Zuta Bamidbar* 10:29.
8. Zevachim 116a.
9. Zevachim 116b.
10. Megila 14b. Imagine the scandal today if the spiritual leader of the Jewish people married the world's best-known prostitute, even after she had converted! But that reflects our own deficiencies, especially our poor understanding of the greatness of spirit of the righteous convert whom Chazal compare to a newborn child (Yevamot 22a), and whose past conduct we are not allowed to remember or mention (Bava Metzia 58b).
11. Megila 14b. Yehoshua did not father any sons – only daughters – so some of his female offspring married *kohanim*.
12. Bamidbar Raba 3:2.
13. Yerushalmi Berachot 2:8.
14. We will need to understand why Yitro and Rachav are linked so frequently in the statements of Chazal.

construed as righteous? We will return to this shortly and attempt to clarify the unique greatness of Rachav.

It is not surprising that the spies naturally gravitated to Rachav's house, and certainly not for licentious purposes. Rachav was well situated to know the thoughts and capabilities of the armies of Canaan, having as she did a close relationship with its kings and officers. Additionally, the Canaanites who had followed the exploits and travails of Israel in the desert knew from Israel's encounter with Bilaam that the "God of Israel hates immorality"[15] and that, in the plains of Moav, Israel had yielded to temptation. The last place the king of Yericho would think to look for Israel's spies would be in a brothel; indeed, it *was* the last place. It was a logical hiding spot, especially considering the identity of these spies.

The Spies
The text of the Navi concealed the identity of the spies, referring to them only as "two men, spies." The Midrash[16] extols their virtues: "No agents were ever as self-sacrificing in attempting to fulfill a dangerous mission as the spies that Yehoshua sent. Who were they? Pinchas and Calev." These two individuals were more than Jewish celebrities; they were distinguished in their righteousness.

Pinchas was the future *kohen gadol* who had zealously protected the honor of Israel in Shittim, by publicly killing Zimri and Cozbi during their very public act of fornication.[17] He would never be suspected of immorality, or of lodging at Rachav's inn for illicit purposes. And Calev was Yehoshua's partner in the ill-fated mission that Moshe dispatched, and together they had resisted the blandishments and conspiracies of the other ten spies.[18] Both were ideal candidates for this mission, and possessed impeccable credentials. But why was this mission necessary altogether?

The Malbim[19] suggests five distinctions between the espionage missions of Moshe and Yehoshua: Moshe sent his spies at the behest of the people whose motivation was not entirely proper, whereas Yehoshua did it on his own initiative. Indeed, the chronology of events would tend to indi-

---

15. Sanhedrin 106a. "The God of this nation hates licentiousness."
16. Bamidbar Raba 16:1.
17. Bamidbar 25:1–9.
18. Bamidbar, Chapters 13–14.
19. Yehoshua 2:1.

cate that Yehoshua sent his spies during the thirty-day mourning period for Moshe, sometime between 7 Adar and 6 Nisan, as the conquest of Yericho occurred on 10 Nisan. It was an opportune moment to send the spies without the knowledge or input of the people who were grieving for the departed Moshe. It also solidified Yehoshua's command. So whereas Moshe succumbed to the will of the people – a failure of leadership – Yehoshua circumvented the people. By the time the mourning period for Moshe ended, Yehoshua had a plan of action to present to his nation.

Furthermore, the Malbim notes, Moshe dispatched them from the wilderness of Sinai, whereas Yehoshua sent them across the Jordan. Pinchas and Calev did not have far to travel and were gone for a very short time. Moshe sent twelve spies, one representing each tribe, as each tribe wanted to know how the land of Israel was suitable for their own specific needs, and whether the land of Israel was worth a war. Moshe directed his agents with the mandate "*v'yaturu et Eretz Canaan*," to scout the land of Israel. The Torah never explicitly called Moshe's agents "spies." They were *tayarim*, tourists in today's lexicon. Yehoshua openly called his agents *meraglim*, spies. A tourist seeks to praise the land, and therefore looks to commend the virtues of the land he visits. Those are the questions for which Moshe sought answers: Are the people strong? Is the land conquerable? Are the cities fortified? Is the land fruitful?[20] The spy, by contrast, looks to expose *ervat ha'aretz*, the weakness of the land, vulnerabilities that an invading army can exploit. The tourist sometimes exaggerates – "the land was too good, the people were giants"; the spy looks for weak points and finds them. In Moshe's time, the question was: *should* they invade. The question for Yehoshua was only: *how* should they invade. Thus, Moshe's spies traversed the entire land of Israel; Yehoshua's spies only went to Yericho, and indeed only to Rachav's house.

Moshe's spies were also dispatched publicly, with pomp and ceremony. Yehoshua's spies were sent secretly by Yehoshua, and as a covert espionage mission, reported directly and exclusively to Yehoshua. "They went in secret, and were told 'make yourselves like deaf-mutes so no one will be aware of your presence. Or pretend to be pottery salesmen, merchants who will attract no attention at all.'"[21]

---

20. Bamidbar 13:18–20.
21. Rashi, Yehoshua 2:1.

This obviously justified Yehoshua's confidence in the ultimate success of the mission. But, if the conquest of the land would be accomplished through miracles, why was the mission authorized in the first place? What information was Yehoshua seeking? We must explore the connection of Rachav to this mission, and why her home became their base of operations.

The Mission

If the spies went to Rachav's inn, it was not because they were seeking information on troop movements, arms depots, or the strengths and weaknesses of Yericho's fortifications. Yehoshua's spies went to Rachav because they sought to gauge the spiritual level of the nation whose land they were about to enter and conquer. Yehoshua endeavored to harmonize the spiritual level of the Jewish people with that of the inhabitants of the land, because until the natives were to be expelled or eliminated the moral climate of the land would greatly influence the Jews themselves. They needed to ascertain whether the Jewish people, as presently constituted, were spiritually compatible with their exalted assignment.[22]

The war of conquest of the land of Israel was not to be won through superior military tactics, but through the superior ethical commitment of the Jewish people to the values of the Torah. "Do not perform the practice of the land of Egypt in which you dwelled, and *do not perform the practice of the land of Canaan to which I bring you...*" (Vayikra 18:3). Who would have a greater insight into the moral level of the people of Canaan than Rachav the harlot? Rachav epitomized the immorality of Canaanite society. *The purpose of the spies' mission was to attempt to subdue and nullify the shell of impurity that typified the Canaanite world – the impurity that the Jewish people were to uproot and eradicate.*[23]

Pinchas and Calev, representing the Jewish people, were tested whether they could resist the allures of Rachav and render the Jewish people worthy of the land of Israel. The spies were sent by Yehoshua "from Shittim" (2:1), the very same place where the Jews years earlier were seduced by the women of Moav – the very event that had prompted Pinchas to kill Zimri, the prince of Israel, and Cozbi, the princess of Midian. In referencing

---

22. *Me'avoor Ha'aretz*, R. Avraham Remer, page 24.
23. *Mishbetzot Zahav*, page 42.

Shittim, the Navi is not merely relating geographical or historical information about the mission, but rather the motivation behind the mission: to re-create the sanctification of God's name that Pinchas and Calev had separately accomplished. Pinchas had personally overcome Israel's attraction to the immorality of Shittim, and Calev had been inoculated against any surrender to immorality through his first trip to Hevron and his inspiration at the graves of the *Avot*.[24]

In the heart of Canaanite immorality, Pinchas and Calev would demonstrate to Rachav the new force in the world that would transform the moral aspirations of mankind: the power of Torah commitment. Indeed, Rachav, naturally, attempted to seduce Pinchas and Calev the very first night they were hidden at her inn. For the first time in her life, Rachav failed, and neither spy was influenced, enticed or even moved by Rachav. Instead, they stood before her like "angels"[25] without any thoughts of sin, and, amazingly, had a profound effect on her. In an instant of moral clarity, Rachav repented. No man had ever resisted her entreaties before, and now two men had arrived at her inn, and showed no interest in her. She sensed in them their abomination of sin, and recognized that there was a purpose in her life beyond providing immediate gratification to men. For the first time, she recognized that the "true pleasure in life, and the enjoyment which surpasses all other enjoyments, is to merit eternal life."[26]

As soon as Pinchas and Calev transformed Rachav the prostitute into Rachav the penitent, they realized that their mission had been accomplished and that Canaanite society would similarly be overturned. If Rachav had been successful in tempting Pinchas or Calev, or had they been unsuccessful in capturing her soul, the conquest of the land could not have proceeded immediately. Yehoshua knew, from bitter experience, that some Jews would have yielded to her charms and thereby jeopardized the entire mission. Instead, through the moral greatness of the spies, the shell of Canaanite immorality was pierced and nullified, and its grip on the world was weakened.

What changed Rachav? Before this encounter, all Rachav knew of the Jewish people was that they were a potent political and military power,

---

24. Rashi, Bamidbar 13:22.
25. Rashi, Yehoshua 2:2.
26. Introduction to *Mesilat Yesharim* of R. Moshe Chaim Luzzatto, as cited by *Mishbetzot Zahav*, page 42.

through ambiguous and indeterminate means. She knew they left Egypt, the Red Sea was miraculously split, they had defeated Sichon, the king of the Emori, and Og, the king of Bashan. She knew all about their military prowess. But now she recognized for the first time that the source of their strength was in their moral strivings. "Some with chariots, and some with horses, but we call out in the name of Hashem, our God" (Tehillim 20:8). She recognized further that the impotence of her customers[27] was not just caused by the fear of the impending conquest by Israel, but by the dampening of the desire for sin caused merely by the proximity of Israel.[28] What a profound influence the Jewish people can have on the world! The simple presence of a holy person, group, or nation elevates the moral level of all whom they contact.[29] The Canaanites knew the Jews were coming, and that alone diminished their ardor for sin. And even Rachav was persuaded to abandon her chosen profession. In the presence of the spiritual might of Israel, they were no longer the same people – spiritually or militarily.

At the moment of her transformation, Rachav merited divine inspiration, and was able to direct the spies to safety and foretell the outcome of their mission. Clearly, like many wicked people, Rachav had tremendous spiritual potential that was latent and never actualized. But when they rectify their path, they can become great *tzadikim*, righteous people with enormous spiritual substance. The greatest *rasha*, wicked person, who possesses great reservoirs of spiritual energy, can become a great *tzadik*, once he is transformed and his energy redirected.[30] Even the tools of promiscuity can be consecrated to a higher purpose: "The same rope and window used by Rachav's customers she used to enable the spies to escape. Rachav

---

27. "We heard, our hearts melted, and because of you our men were dispirited' (2:11) and Zevachim 116a.
28. *Mishbetzot Zahav*, page 47.
29. The Alter of Slobodka, R. Natan Tzvi Finkel, was quoted as saying that he could not guarantee that his disciples would never sin, but he could guarantee that they would never enjoy their sins. The influence of holiness extends far beyond its immediate vicinity, and that indeed is the eternal calling of the Jewish people – to be the catalyst for holiness and morality in the world.
30. The Maharal explains that this is the intent of the Gemara (Gittin 57b) that states: "Some of Haman's descendants learned Torah in Bnei Brak, some of Sisera's descendants taught Torah to children in Yerushalayim, etc." The source of great evil has the potential to become the source of an even greater good.

said to God: 'With these I sinned, so with these, forgive me.'"[31] No person could be as immoral as Rachav was – most of us do not have the time or energy. Yet, when she was transformed, Rachav merited *Ruach HaKodesh*, divine inspiration, and eventually married Yehoshua himself. If the task of the Jewish people is to bring the nations to acknowledge the sovereignty of God in the world, then Rachav represented the ultimate conquest of the Jewish idea – someone recognized by non-Jewish society as the antithesis of morality, who was then elevated through the attainment of ideas and virtues to the highest stratum of the Jewish people, the ancestress of prophets.

In that accomplishment, she duplicated the role of Yitro, the priest of Midian and Moshe's father-in-law, who abandoned his idolatrous past, and represented the presence of the non-Jewish world joined to the Jewish people in service of God. Thus, we have found that Rachav and Yitro are linked conceptually by Chazal several times, as Rachav was the follower and natural successor of Yitro.[32]

Precursor to Conquest

The question that remains is: why is it necessary for the Jewish people to have a land that we call our own, a land that has to be conquered and constantly defended? Many religions operate without a land of their own. Christianity today lacks a particular land; Islam, it seems, lays claim to everyone's land. But why must Jews have a land that is uniquely ours? We have Shabbat, *kashrut*, laws of family purity, prayer and the study of Torah. So why do we also require a land for our ethical message to go forth to mankind?

Our return to the land of Israel is not merely an event of geopolitical interest, but is primarily designed to inspire the world and further its moral development. The whole purpose of the Torah – its chronology from the selection of Avraham through the death of Moshe – was to create the Jewish people and bring them, equipped with the laws of the Torah, into the land of Israel where they would establish a model society. That is why Chazal state[33] "the only indispensable books of Tanach are the Five Books of Moshe and the Book of Yehoshua" – the Torah for its laws, and the Book

---

31. Rashi, Yehoshua 2:15.
32. See above, and notes 10 and 11.
33. Nedarim 22b.

of Yehoshua because it describes the conquest and division of the land of Israel. With the Jewish people residing in the land of Israel observing the Torah, the goal of creation itself was fulfilled and the Torah found its natural culmination.

The Jewish people were not bequeathed the land of Israel for its diamonds, crops or material bounty,[34] but because we yearn to perfect the world, and the land of Israel is the foundation from which our message goes forth to the world. Our fondest desire is *tikun olam*, world perfection, and that is not possible as long as mankind is gripped by passions – aggression, materialism, corruption, and the unrestrained pursuit of man's baser instincts. Our task is to convey to the world the appropriate answers to the spiritual dilemmas of life – the purpose of our existence, the correct way to live, the timeless moral norms of the Creator, and the true ideas of God. This mandate can only be optimally fulfilled when we dwell on our land in peace and security, as a "kingdom of priests and a holy nation" (Shemot 19:6).[35]

We have the answers to mankind's questions, and the cure to what ails them. But as long as we are unaware or unworthy of our mission, and as long as mankind is incessantly drawn after its materialistic passions, the realization of that mission will be delayed and mankind's misery will be prolonged. We are the "world's heart" (*Kuzari*) and the "world's intellect" (*Zohar*); we are the nation that provides the world with its spiritual substance.[36] For these tasks, the land of Israel serves as our headquarters, and our original entry into the land was designed to be the precursor of the Messianic era. As the *Zohar* states: "Had Moshe succeeded in bringing us *into* the land of Israel, the Temple would have been built immediately without any possibility of destruction or exile."[37] But Moshe sinned at the waters of Meriva and we never fully embraced our mission, and that historical era still awaits.

When the spies left from Shittim – the place of immorality – and emerged from the house of Rachav chaste, pure in body and soul, Yehoshua

---

34. See Sotah 14a in reference to Moshe's desires to enter the land of Israel.
35. *Me'avoor Ha'aretz*, page 24.
36. *Kuzari*, Part 2, Chapter 36; *Zohar*, Shemot, page 108b; found in *Me'avoor Ha'aretz*, page 24.
37. *Zohar*, Pinchas 220b, cited in *Michtav Me'Eliyahu* of Rav Eliyahu Dessler, vol. 2, page 22.

recognized that the conquest of the land of Israel was at hand. They entered a brothel, and emerged not with the world's most infamous prostitute but with a future convert and a penitent. The Jewish nation was ready to proceed to its destiny.

The Sign
The spies asked Rachav to suspend the scarlet thread from her window, as a sign of their mutual covenant.

> Behold – when we come into this land, you shall bind this scarlet cord in the window from which you lowered us, and your father, mother, brothers and all your father's household shall you gather to you in the house. Then it shall be that anyone who leaves the doors of your house for the outside, his blood guilt shall be on his own head; we will be clean; but anyone who will be with you inside the house, his blood guilt shall be on our head, if a hand is upon him… And she said "Like your words, so it is," and she sent them away, and she tied the scarlet cord to the window (Yehoshua 2:17–21).

What was the significance of this scarlet thread?

The scarlet thread was featured in the divine service in the Temple on Yom Kippurim. The thread was tied to the scapegoat sent into the wilderness, and the thread turned white as an indication that the sins of the Jewish people were forgiven. "Come, let us reason together, says God. If your sins are like scarlet, they will become white like snow, and if red as crimson, they will become as wool" (Yeshayahu 1:18). The scarlet thread is a symbol of contrition and repentance.

But there is an earlier reference in the Torah to a scarlet thread. After Yosef was sold, Yaakov's son Yehuda "sinned" with his ex-daughter-in-law Tamar and she became pregnant with twins.

> And it happened that as she gave birth, one put out a hand; the midwife took a scarlet thread and tied it on his hand saying, "This one came out first!" And it was as he drew back his hand, that behold, his brother emerged. And she said, "with what strength have you asserted yourself!" And he called his name Peretz. And then his brother emerged, on whose hand was the scarlet thread, and he called his name Zerach. (Breisheet 38:28–30)

Why does it matter who emerged first, and that the first child wore a scarlet thread on his hand? Because Yehuda was the ancestor of the royal house of Israel, and his firstborn would be the progenitor of the Moshiach. The Messiah will be a descendant of Peretz and not Zerach, and so that is duly noted here. The Midrash Hagadol[38] asserts that Yehoshua's spies were, indeed, Peretz and Zerach. Of course, this is not meant literally. Rather, Chazal taught that Yehoshua's spies catalyzed the Messianic process that began with the birth of Peretz, by hastening our conquest of the land of Israel. This infantile struggle between Peretz and Zerach symbolized the suddenness of redemption, bursting into the open, and propelling past the scarlet thread – just as Peretz leaped ahead of his "older" brother Zerach.

The spies Pinchas and Calev told Rachav to put the scarlet thread, the symbol of redemption and royalty, on her window. It is a sign that the Jewish people have returned home, and the Messianic process is advancing, and all who wish to share in that glorious venture are welcome.

When the Jewish people adhere to the moral standards of the Torah, we assume a different dimension of existence. We become worthy not only of the blessings of the Torah and the conquest of the land of Israel, but also of the coming of Moshiach and the ultimate national existence as faithful servants of the Creator.

Summary

Yehoshua's goal, and the substance of his plan, was to assess the spiritual state of Canaan, and ascertain whether they were ready for the invasion of the Jewish idea. Rachav was the test case, and her acceptance of the Torah confirmed the imminence of the conquest.

When the Jewish people are worthy, then the world will recognize us as God's agents and the moral force that He intended us to be. Then our conquest of the land will be complete, our settlement will be secure and uncontested, and God's plan for mankind will be realized.

---

38. Midrash Hagadol Chayei Sarah, page 371, cited in *Mishbetzot Zahav*, page 53, quoting from the work *L'Michseh Atik*.

Chapter Two
CROSSING THE JORDAN

Israel's miraculous crossing of the Jordan River is joyously extolled every time we recite Hallel: "The sea saw and fled, the Jordan turned backward" (Tehillim 114:3). Although Rashi and Ibn Ezra note here that this refers to the splitting of all the waters of the world – including the Jordan – as part of the miracle at the Red Sea,[1] Radak and the Malbim disagree and explicitly relate this phrase to the splitting of the Jordan River during Yehoshua's time. Here too, like at the Red Sea, a miracle took place. On 10 Nisan, the river split, and the Jewish people walked past a column of water on dry land and entered the land of Israel.

What exactly happened? What is the difference between the splitting of the Red Sea and the splitting of the Jordan? And, perhaps of greater interest, *why* did the Jewish people have to enter Israel in such a grand fashion? Why did they not simply cross via a ferry or a pontoon bridge? Why not simply wade across? After all, the Jordan River is one of the least impressive bodies of water in the world, resembling a creek more than a river.[2] Certainly, the miracle at the Red Sea is much more famous. Not only was the Red Sea more difficult to traverse, but the miracle there also enabled the Jews to escape certain death at the hands of the advancing Egyptians.

1. In accordance with the opinion of Shmuel, cited by Rav Yehuda, that Hallel celebrates the Exodus, and was first recited by Moshe and the prophets of the time after crossing the Red Sea (Pesachim 117a).
2. When he first viewed the Jordan River, Henry Kissinger allegedly exclaimed: "This is it? It shows what can be accomplished with good public relations."

Why was it necessary, so to speak, for Hashem to repeat this miracle for this generation of Jews? Other questions emerge from the verses.

> Yehoshua arose early in the morning, and they traveled from Shittim and came to the Jordan, he and all the children of Israel, and they lodged there before they crossed. (Yehoshua 3:1)

Why was it necessary to state that they lodged there before crossing? What is the relevance to the events at hand?

> It was at the end of three days that the officers circulated in the midst of the camp. They commanded the people saying, "When you see the Ark of the Covenant of God, and the *kohanim*, the Levites, carrying it, then you shall move from your place and follow it. But there shall be a distance between yourselves and it – a measure of two thousand cubits – do not approach any closer to it, so that you may know the way in which you should go, for you have not passed this way yesterday or the day before." Yehoshua said to the people, "Prepare yourselves, for tomorrow God will do wonders in your midst."[3] Yehoshua then spoke to the *kohanim* saying, "Carry the Ark of the Covenant and pass before the people," so they carried the Ark of the Covenant and went before the people. (Yehoshua 3:2–6)

Several parallels connect this passage with the revelation at Sinai. Yitro, Moshe's father-in-law, admonished him[4] to appoint a council to assist him in governance, so Moshe could focus on imparting to the people "the way in which they should go."[5] Moshe commanded the people as a prelude to the Revelation, "let them be prepared for the third day,"[6] to sanctify themselves appropriately. And in both places, the anticipated events occurred after three days.

Additionally, Yehoshua curiously instructed the *kohanim* to carry the *Aron HaKodesh*, and not the Levites whose task it was in the wilderness

---

3. This verse begins our *haftara* for the first day of Pesach, the first Yom Tov that occurs after 10 Nisan when these events occurred.
4. Before the Revelation, at least according to the traditional chronology of the Torah.
5. "*Et haderech yeilchu vah*," Shemot 18:20, almost identical to the phrase used here in 3:4.
6. "*V'kidashtam hayom u'machar*," Shemot 19:10, similar to Yehoshua's charge "*Hitkadashu*" in Yehoshua 3:5.

to carry the sacred objects of the *Mishkan*, the Tabernacle, including the Holy Ark.[7] Why did Yehoshua change the procedures?

The Gemara Sotah (33b–34a) elaborates on this latter point:

> How did Israel cross the Jordan? During the wilderness years, the Ark traveled behind two tribal banners, but on this day it traveled in front. As it says, "behold the Ark of the Covenant of the Master of the whole earth is passing before you in the Jordan…" [Yehoshua 3:12]. During the wilderness years, the Levites carried the Ark, but on this day the *kohanim* carried it. And this was one of three times the *kohanim* carried the Ark instead of the Levites.[8]

Apparently, this was done with forethought. So what message was Yehoshua sending by having the *kohanim* carry the Ark?

The story continues:

> And God said to Yehoshua: "Today I will begin to exalt you in the eyes of all Israel, that they may know that just as I was with Moshe, so will I be with you. You shall command the *kohanim*, bearers of the Ark of the Covenant, saying, 'When you come to the edge of the waters of the Jordan, you shall stand in the Jordan.'"
>
> Yehoshua said to the children of Israel: "Come here and listen to the words of the Lord, your God." And Yehoshua said, "Through this you will know that the Living God is in your midst, and He will surely drive away from before you the [seven Canaanite nations]. Behold the Ark of the Covenant…is passing before you in the Jordan. And now, take for yourselves twelve men, one from each of the tribes of Israel. And it shall be that as the soles of the feet of the *kohanim*, bearers of the Ark of God, rest in the waters of the Jordan, the waters of the Jordan will be cut off – the waters that descend from upstream – and they will stand as one column" (Yehoshua 3:7–13).

Again, the Gemara Sotah (34a) underscores this point: "As soon as the *kohanim* dipped their feet in the Jordan, the waters flowed backward and stood in one column, at a height of 12 *mil* by 12 *mil*, corresponding to the dimensions of the camp of Israel." The water which here stood in one column was in contrast to the Red Sea, where the water formed two walls on opposite sides of the people as they crossed. Indeed, "the water descending

---

7. Bamidbar 4:1–16.
8. The others being when the Jewish people circled Yericho and when the Ark was brought into the Temple of Shlomo (Sotah 33b).

from upstream stood still and they rose up in one column… and the water that descends to the Sea of the Plain, the Dead Sea, ceased and was cut off, and the people crossed opposite Yericho" (3:15–16). And even though the waters flowing from the north stopped, the waters did not overflow the banks of the Jordan. At the Red Sea, the very nature of water changed, as it stood in two walls and dry land materialized between these walls. At the Jordan, the water remained in its original form; the miracle was in the cessation of its flow, after which the dry ground emerged naturally. In that sense, the crossing of the Jordan necessitated a "smaller" miracle than the crossing of the Red Sea, for reasons which will shortly become clear.

The Memorial of the Stones

> The *kohanim*… stood firmly on dry ground, in the middle of the Jordan, and all Israel crossed on the dry land, until the entire nation finished crossing the Jordan. (Yehoshua 3:17)

After they crossed, Yehoshua commanded the previously designated twelve men, one from each tribe, to each take a stone from the river, bring it to their lodging place for the night (in Gilgal), and set it there.

> So this will be a sign in your midst, when your children ask tomorrow, saying, "what are these stones to you?" And you shall tell them, "that the waters of the Jordan were cut off before the Ark of the Covenant of Hashem – when it crossed the Jordan, the waters of the Jordan were cut off – and these stones shall be a remembrance for the Children of Israel forever." (Yehoshua 4:6–7)

In addition, Yehoshua himself took twelve stones and set them himself in the Jordan River as another monument to the miraculous crossing. "On that day, Hashem exalted Yehoshua in the eyes of all Israel and they revered him as they had revered Moshe all the days of his life" (4:14). As soon as the *kohanim* exited the river, the waters returned to their normal flow. At Gilgal, Yehoshua erected the stones taken from the Jordan by the tribal leaders and proclaimed that this memorial was an eternal reminder that "Hashem dried up the waters of the Jordan before you until you crossed, as He did to the Red Sea, which He dried up before us until we crossed. So that all the peoples of the earth would know the hand of Hashem, so that you would fear Hashem all your days" (4:23–24).

Why were all these wonders necessary? Rashi (on 3:9) states that when Yehoshua urged the people to "draw near and hear the words of Hashem," it means that "he compressed them between the two staves of the Holy Ark, one of the places in *Tanach* in which the small was able to contain the great."[9] What does this mean?

Why did they have to suddenly deviate from the routine of forty years, in which the *Aron HaKodesh* traveled first, followed by Yehuda, Reuven, etc.? Why send the Ark first, and why send it with the *kohanim*? And why did the Ark have to travel two thousand cubits in front of the people (3:4)?

Why does Yehoshua use the expression "with this you will know that *the Living God* is in your midst" (3:10)? This is the first time in *Tanach* such an expression is used.[10] What does it mean, and why is it employed here?

Two different expressions regarding the nationhood of Israel are also used here, for some emphasis. In 4:1, "it happened when the entire *nation* (*goy*) crossed," while in 4:11 it states "it happened when the entire *people* (*am*) crossed." What is the distinction between a *goy* and an *am*?

Furthermore, Gemara Sotah (35b) notes that there were *three* sets of stones assembled: one by Moshe in Moav, one by Yehoshua in the middle of the Jordan (4:8), and one set by Yehoshua in Gilgal. Why do we need any physical monuments, much less three? And a fascinating Midrash states that the stones on which Yaakov rested his head as he was fleeing his brother Esav and the land of Israel to go to his uncle Lavan – the night he had the vision of the angels – were the same stones that the tribal leaders extracted from the Jordan.[11] What is the symbolism of that Midrash?

Rashi (4:11) states that after the Jews crossed, the *kohanim* stepped out of the water and the river resumed its flow, the *kohanim* and the Ark were actually on the *eastern* bank of the Jordan – directly opposite the location of Yehoshua and the people. So how did they cross? "The Ark lifted them across, and they passed over." Radak remarks that, if this is so, this is as great as any other miracle and should have been recorded in the

---

9. "*Tzimtzaim et kulam*," similar, in a sense, to Elisha's flask of oil which miraculously contained far more than it could have contained.
10. "*El Chai.*"
11. *Mishbetzot Zahav*, page 68, quoting the *Zohar* on Parshat Vayetzei (1:72).

text itself!¹² Why didn't the *kohanim* just exit on the western bank of the Jordan – like everyone else?

It emerges that there were a number of miracles here: the *kohanim* stood in the water, the water stopped flowing, stones were removed from the river by the tribal leaders and by Yehoshua – who erected his stones *in the river*, and the *kohanim* flew across the river with the *Aron HaKodesh*. There is much symbolism here, and dramatic undercurrents. What is happening that, on this momentous day, will confirm our claim to the land of Israel? And isn't it interesting that the day on which we entered Israel – 10 Nisan – a day anticipated since the time of Avraham – is not commemorated or celebrated at all by the Jewish people?¹³ So what is it about the miraculous crossing of the Jordan River that resonates with Jews until today, that was recorded by King David in Hallel?

The Red Sea and the Jordan River

We must understand the differences between the splitting of the Red Sea and the splitting of the Jordan River. At the Red Sea, the waters were raging and the Egyptians were chasing the Jewish people, who were in complete panic mode. According to the most famous description of the events, the leader of the tribe of Yehuda, Nachshon ben Aminadav, jumped into the sea in a leap of faith, and the sea split. Others say that the sea did not split until Nachshon was in the water up to his neck, at which point he pleaded with Hashem: "Save me, Lord, for the waters have reached until my soul" (Tehillim 69:2), or that it was the entire tribe of Binyamin that jumped into the waters.¹⁴

The common denominator was that some representative of the Jewish people had to physically enter the Red Sea, before the water divided and the salvation commenced. And this took place amid absolute pandemonium, with groups of Jews arguing with Moshe – some wishing to proceed, oth-

---

12. Yet, this point – "*Aron noseh et nosav*" – that the Ark carries its bearers – is the source of the *halacha* that was the downfall of Uzza (II Shmuel 6:6) when he unnecessarily reached out to steady the Ark as it *seemed* to be falling. "The Ark carries its bearers! It certainly can carry itself!" (Sotah 35a).
13. And even if we would not celebrate this day because it was just the *beginning* of the conquest and not the conclusion, it is still noteworthy that we do not even acknowledge this day at all.
14. Sotah 36b–37a.

ers to return to Egypt, and others wishing to fight the Egyptians.[15] At the Red Sea, the Jewish people themselves were riven by strife and dissension, so divided that Chazal state that the Jews crossed over twelve separate "bridges" – one for each tribe.[16] Each tribe crossed by itself. And the Red Sea was caused to split by a "powerful east wind through the night," brought about after Moshe raised his staff over the sea (Shemot 14:21).

The splitting of the Jordan River was almost the complete opposite. There was no rage, panic or divisiveness. There was no tumult, and the text emphasized that "the feet of the *kohanim* would *come to rest* in the water…" (Yehoshua 3:13) – serenely and placidly.[17] At the Jordan, all Jews crossed as one – "all Israel crossing on dry ground until the entire nation finished crossing the Jordan" (3:17).[18] At the Red Sea, the Jews were not prepared for the miracle; they were abruptly told "let them journey forth" (Shemot 14:15).[19] They were not even told that the sea would split! Here, the people had several months earlier been informed by Moshe that they would cross the Jordan miraculously,[20] and Yehoshua notified them the day before of the great wonders that would occur (Yehoshua 3:5). The people spent that night leisurely at a hotel at the east bank of the Jordan River; no one was chasing them; and the next night – after the crossing – they went to another inn, this time on the west bank of the Jordan River. All in all, a peaceful, relaxing way to enter the land of Israel – the opposite of the Red Sea crossing which was frenzied and frantic.

What changed? Sinai changed everything. The splitting of the Red Sea occurred before the Giving of the Torah, and was due to the self-sacrifice of Nachshon and the others. The only merit of the people was their willingness to relinquish their lives for Hashem, by marching into the Red Sea at His word. But the Jews entered the land of Israel with the merit of the Torah, and indeed, the Torah literally preceded them into the land.[21]

The Torah must be supreme in the land of Israel, and even the land

15. Shemot 14:10–14.
16. Midrash Shemot Raba 24:1, Rambam on Avot 5:4.
17. "*K'noach kapot raglei hakohanim.*"
18. "*Ad asher tamu kol hagoy…*"
19. "*Vi'yisa'u*" – as if it were natural that they should just march into the sea!
20. "For you are crossing the Jordan to come and possess the land that Hashem, your God, gives you…" (Devarim 11:31). Rashi there quotes the Sifrei that "the miracles of the Jordan will be a sign to you that you should enter and conquer the land."
21. *Mishbetzot Zahav*, page 65.

of Israel must defer to the will of the Torah. We are unlike other peoples that conquer a land, and then imbue that land with their own culture, values and personality. We entered the land of Israel with the Torah – the fundamental framework of Jewish national life and our definitive quality as a people. That is why the *kohanim* stood with the *Aron HaKodesh* in the middle of the Jordan River, and why the nation had to pass by the *Aron HaKodesh* as their entry to the land. The land and the people must always be subordinate to the Torah, the primary value in Jewish life – basically, the opposite of the secular Zionist ethos.

This concept explains Rashi's statement that he "compressed them between the two staves of the Holy Ark" in order to listen to the words of Hashem. Our claim to the land of Israel is based on the notion that we constitute one bloc – one body and one soul – in the acceptance of the Torah[22] and that the parameters of our national life are the two staves of the Holy Ark. In a real sense, our national boundaries are the walls of the Holy Ark – and safeguarding those boundaries preserves the physical borders of the land of Israel.

The Torah was not given to individuals but to the entire Jewish people, and every single Jew. That is the meaning of "*kol yisrael arevin zeh lazeh,*" that all Jews are guarantors for one another.[23] If even one Jew had refused to accept the Torah, we would not have been worthy to receive it as a people. Thus, in our prayers we ask that Hashem should bless us *kulanu k'echad*, "all as one, with the light of Your countenance,"[24] or *v'nizkeh chulanu*, "may we all together speedily merit His light."[25] Together, as one.

So, too, every Jew has to accept the gift of the land of Israel. If even one Jew contests our right to the land of Israel, then our claim is diluted and our very worthiness questioned. Certainly, the last century and the last decade have proven this proposition. Whenever Jews renounce our rights to the land – in whole or in part – our claim becomes more tenuous and our enemies are emboldened and strengthened in their evil designs. We cannot fully grasp either the Torah or the land of Israel unless every Jew accepts both entirely.[26]

22. "Like one person with one heart," Rashi, Shemot 19:2.
23. Shevuot 39a.
24. End of *Shemoneh Esrei*.
25. End of first *bracha* before *Kriat Shema*.
26. *Mishbetzot Zahav*, page 61, citing the *Sefer Chasidim* (233).

Our possession of the land must also be perceived as exclusive, or it will not endure. "While they were still in the Jordan, Yehoshua said to them: 'Know why you are crossing the Jordan – it is on condition that you drive out the inhabitants of the land before you… If you do this, well and good; otherwise, this water will return and inundate me and you'" (Sotah 34a). Sharing the land with other nations dilutes its spiritual character, weakens our ability to establish a Torah society, and ultimately undermines our existence there. In the metaphor of the *Zohar*,[27] the tribal leaders removed from the Jordan the very stones on which Yaakov rested the night he fled from his brother and encountered the heavenly angels. It was the night on which the promise of the land exclusively to the seed of Yaakov – and not Esav nor Lavan – was confirmed.

The Jewish national life is bordered by the staves of the *Aron HaKodesh*, and every aspect of Jewish life has to fit within those poles – or it will surely fail. The physical boundaries of the land of Israel are inherently linked to the spiritual boundaries signified by the poles of the Holy Ark. When we cherish and safeguard what is contained within the Holy Ark, we preserve and fortify our physical possession of the land itself. Thus, in Rashi's expression, the "small" – the area between the staves – can contain "the many" – the myriads of the Jewish people.

The miraculous crossing of the Jordan River defined the Torah as the very foundation of our conquest and settlement of the land of Israel, in a way that was unforgettable. That is why there were three sets of stones used to ratify this idea: before the Jews crossed the Jordan (Moshe's stones), while the Jews were in the Jordan (Yehoshua's stones), and the stones set up at Gilgal on the very first night we lodged as a people in the land of Israel.[28] It was the merit of the Torah that gave us the land of Israel, and only the merit of the Torah would enable us to retain it.

Each set of stones reflected a different fundamental principle of Judaism. Maharsha[29] cites the three pillars of Judaism as enunciated by Rav Yosef Albo in the *Sefer HaIkkarim*: that Hashem created the world, that Hashem gave the Torah to the Jewish people, and that Hashem ordained a system of reward and punishment – a reflection of the involvement of

---

27. See note 11 above.
28. Sotah 35b.
29. Maharsha on Sotah 35b.

Hashem in human affairs. Moshe's stones in the plains of Moav corresponded to the covenant of Torah; Yehoshua's stones in the Jordan – and its miraculous splitting – testified to Hashem as Creator and Lord of nature; and the stones of Gilgal symbolized the system of reward and punishment that would be the basis of our rights to the land of Israel.

These stones were, literally, the cornerstones of our settlement of the land, and the national charter that greeted every visitor to the land of Israel. Every country has a symbol or seal that identifies the country in the popular mind and is prominently displayed at its border crossings. Israel must be identified as the land of Torah, and its people must proudly proclaim to all the three cardinal principles: the divine creation, the divine origin of the Torah, and Divine Providence. These stones are our border monuments.

This is why the Torah is referred to consistently here in these two chapters of Yehoshua as the *Aron Brit Hashem* – the Ark of the Covenant of Hashem. The entry into the land required the reinforcement of the covenant between Hashem and the Jewish people, symbolized by the Torah. Thus, the Ark marched first across the Jordan, and not behind two banners as in the wilderness, and the *kohanim* – the sub-division of the tribe of Levi primarily responsible for divine service and for the continuity of Torah – were mandated to carry the *Aron HaKodesh* here, and not other *Levi'im*.[30] The tribe of Levi generally carried the Ark only in the wilderness, but only the *kohanim* were authorized to carry the Ark within the borders of Israel.[31]

The Jewish people's covenant with Hashem carries two implications.[32] A covenant is firstly a divine creation, which flows from Hashem to us and therefore can never change. The Torah never states that the Jewish people covenanted with Hashem; rather, Hashem enacted a covenant with His people, our fathers and ourselves. Chazal[33] can therefore state that the "*merit* of our fathers has ceased" but not the "*covenant* with our fathers." Their merit is rooted in their illustrious deeds, which reflect well on their descendants but can nevertheless be exhausted by subsequent events. But

---

30. "For the lips of a *kohen* should safeguard knowledge, and they should seek the Torah from his mouth…" (Malachi 2:7).
31. Rambam, *Sefer HaMitzvot*, Mitzvat Aseh 34, cited by *Mishbetzot Zahav*, page 55.
32. *Me'avoor Ha'aretz*, page 34, quoting Rav Zvi Yehuda HaKohen Kook.
33. Tosafot, "*U'shmuel amar*," Shabbat 55a.

the covenant can never be consumed, as it flows from Hashem's word, which is eternal and unchanging.

A covenant is secondly a "bond of life" between Hashem and man, and reminds us that Hashem is never remote or distant from us. The covenant is vibrant, not dormant; it is present, not past. This is the meaning of the expression *El Chai* – the "Living God" – that Yehoshua employs (3:10). This phrase is also used at a *brit mila* in the blessing after the *brit*,[34] because at that moment, we demonstrate our fidelity to the covenant – which is an active relationship between Hashem and the Jewish people. We do not relate to Hashem solely for historical reasons, i.e., because He once took us out of Egypt and once gave us the Torah. We have an existing, living relationship with Hashem. That is *El Chai*, and the Jews were so informed by Yehoshua while entering the land of Israel: You are not terminating your connection with Hashem and entering a world free of Torah; you are rather entering a world in which the Torah will come to life in all its fullness, and Hashem's presence will be manifest.

The bond of the covenant links the material forces that are intrinsically distant from Hashem, and draws the divine light from its divine source into the physical realms. This phenomenon occurs to the greatest extent in the land of Israel. It is more than a blessed land, or the land chosen by Hashem for His chosen people. The land of Israel is the tableau on which the word of Hashem will be animated, and from there spread forth to the rest of mankind. Israel has hills, mountains, valleys, farms and crops like all lands, but its unique dimension is the divine covenant – the reinforcement of Hashem's involvement with the world of man.[35] Our Sages therefore state that all blessing to the world is filtered through the land of Israel and specifically through Yerushalayim, a fulfillment of Hashem's promise to Avraham that "through you, the families of the earth will be blessed" (Breisheet 12:3). Yerushalayim is the light of the world, through which the rest of the world receives its illumination.[36]

The conquest of the land of Israel was a reminder that the Creator of the world is also the Master of the Covenant, and that the land of Israel is not mundane territory but is inherently sanctified. Before we entered the

---

34. "*Al ken bischar zot* El Chai *chelkenu tzurenu.*"
35. *Me'avoor Ha'aretz*, page 35.
36. Midrash Breisheet Raba 59:5.

land, the Torah always marched two thousand cubits ahead of the people, with two tribes intervening, for the Torah was a distant guide that could not be fully implemented – as it cannot be anywhere in the exile. Once we entered the land of Israel that distance evaporated, the Torah could be fully actualized, and the covenant became our natural state of existence. This is the recognition implicit in *El Chai*, that the "Living God" is apparent in our lives, and there is no barrier between the people, the land and the Torah. The Torah itself comes to life through the people and the land.

That is why the crossing of the Jordan River involved a "lesser" miracle – merely the halt of the water's flow. When we crossed the Red Sea, nature itself was shattered. "The sea saw and fled…" (Tehillim 114:3). The waters of the Red Sea formed "a wall, on their left and on their right" (Shemot 14:22). But when we crossed the Jordan, nature was elevated, not shattered. The waters rose up as one column, "the Jordan turned backward" (Tehillim 114:3). It turned in order to demonstrate that a new existence was coming into being. At the Red Sea, the natural order was negated, "and Israel saw the great hand that Hashem wielded against Egypt, and the people revered Hashem and they believed in Hashem and in his servant Moshe" (Shemot 14:31). Now, nature would no longer be negated by the might of Hashem but consecrated by the accomplishments of His people. As we entered the land of Israel, the Jews were taught that both nature and the miraculous – *teva* and *nes* – are part of the same creation and emerge from the same Source. In Israel, our mandate is to sanctify the physical until the Torah completely permeates the land.

In the wilderness, the Torah's applicability to all realms of life was limited, but Moshe's spies did not see it that way. Rather, they felt that the highest level of spiritual existence could be found only in the desert directly under the watchful eye of Hashem. They felt that the land of Israel was too sacred for farming, building, commerce and mundane life; they did not want the holy Torah to be "degraded" into a system of agricultural, civil and criminal laws. For Moshe's spies, the desert life was ideal. This error was a grievous distortion of Torah, and necessitated their downfall and the Jewish people's extended wandering in the wilderness in order to prepare them to fully embrace the Torah.[37]

Consequently, the Torah entered the Jordan River itself in front of the

---

37. *Me'avoor Ha'aretz*, page 47.

people; the people passed by it and entered the land first *without* the Torah. "It comes out that the Ark and the *kohanim* were on one (the east) side, and the people were on one (the west) side" (Sotah 35a). The Torah then miraculously crossed the river, in order to emphasize to the people that their bond with the land was not inherent but was always subject to the dictates of the Torah which came from a different dimension of existence.

The classic mistake of our forefathers that led to the exile was the notion that the land of Israel belongs to the Jewish people inherently, and the Torah was just a set of good ideas that we can accept or reject as we wish, without consequence. That notion was the death knell of Jewish sovereignty in the land of Israel, and therefore the Torah entered Israel in a supernatural way to impress upon the people this cornerstone of our national life. Here, the people entered the land – but did not move forward until the Torah came across, sweeping down with the *kohanim* as if on a magic carpet, and reminding the people of the terms of their entry, settlement and possession of the land. Indeed, perhaps the people were given a momentary sense of the emptiness of life in a land of Israel that is bereft of Torah.

The land of Israel introduced us to an existence that was beyond nature. There are two types of miracles. One defies nature, like the splitting of the Red Sea or the Jordan. But there is a second type of "miracle" which does not defy nature but rather transcends it.[38] This second quality defines our life in the land of Israel until today; our settlement transcends nature, politics, diplomacy and the natural history of nations. How does one lamb survive among seventy wolves? Or among two hundred wolves? Israel is the only member state of the United Nations whose demise is actively plotted by other member states which are tacitly abetted by still others. Its numerical and material inferiority compared to its sworn enemies remains astonishing, and yet is casually accepted. But it is not purely natural.

The *Aron* and the *Luchot* also transcended nature,[39] and did not require dry land either to cross the river or to carry its bearers across. As this was the permanent state of the *Aron HaKodesh*, this miracle did not require any special mention in the text. This entry did, however, forever characterize the nature of our possession of the land – a people, a land and a Torah.

---

38. *Michtav Me'Eliyahu*, Rav Eliyahu Dessler, vol. 4, page 260.
39. Bava Batra 99a.

That is why the Jewish people were first termed by Yehoshua a *goy* (nation) before the *Aron* crossed and then an *am* (people) after the *Aron* crossed. The etymology of *goy* derives from the word *g'viya* – body. A *goy* has a purely physical connection; the members of the nation are connected to each other and to their land. This was our relationship with the land after we crossed but before the Torah entered the land. We were one *guf*, one body, but without any other intrinsic association. But after the *Aron* crossed and the Torah crossed the threshold of the land of Israel, we fully became an *am* – a people, from the word *im* (with), together as one people with one mandate.[40]

The modern return to Israel occurred without the foundation of Torah, and therefore with all the attendant consequences apparent today. It is only in the last few decades that the Torah has gained new vigor in Israel, but still has not pervaded large sectors of the Jewish public. In other words, the land of Israel in our day was re-conquered by a *goy*, not by an *am* – a *goy* who focused on the physical renaissance and development of the land. The nation bonded with the land and the desert blossomed. But the ties of a *goy* – rooted in the material – will necessarily fray over time, as, in fact, has happened. The deeper relationship is that of an *am* – a nation that has a metaphysical purpose to its existence and does not simply occupy space between defined physical borders. The modern realization of the Jewish people in Israel as an *am* still awaits us.

The miraculous crossing of the Jordan was designed to establish the proper balance between the people, land and Torah. There are always two potential dangers when that balance is upset – perhaps the people will not be able to rejuvenate the land and infuse it with the breadth of Torah, or perhaps the land will be vibrant and produce an overflowing bounty, and we will perceive Israel primarily as the land of diamonds, oranges and high tech. These dangers always accompany our sojourn in the land of Israel, until today.[41]

How did Yehoshua seek to counter these forces? In the next chapter (Yehoshua 5), Yehoshua reintroduced the people to the *mitzva* of *mila* (circumcision) and the preparations for *The Korban Pesach*, which came just four days after their entry into the land. Neither *mitzva* had been observed

---

40. *Me'avoor Ha'aretz*, page 48.
41. *Me'avoor Ha'aretz*, page 48.

during the last thirty-eight years in the wilderness.[42] Yehoshua informed them of the *mitzva* of *chadash*, and the use of the new grain after the offering of the *omer* on 16 Nisan. The *mon* (manna) from Heaven stopped falling, and the supernatural daily existence ended. *Mila, Pesach, chadash* and other *mitzvot* began the process of implementation of the Torah system, on both individual and national levels.

On this day – 10 Nisan – to commemorate these events, Yehoshua composed and ordained the second blessing of Birkat HaMazon.[43] "We thank You, Hashem, because You have given to our forefathers as a heritage a desirable, good and spacious land…"[44] This was a momentous day in Jewish history – the fulfillment of the aspirations of Avraham, Yitzchak, Yaakov, Yosef, Moshe and Aharon, as well as the realization of the promise of the *Brit Bein HaBetarim*,[45] Hashem's promise to Avraham.

The miracles at the Jordan sent an intimidating message to the nations of the world – that they should fear Hashem and His people – and an awesome reminder to the Jewish people of the wonders that Hashem performed for us.[46] The reminders would be necessary but insufficient, as again and again we strayed from our divinely ordained mission. Our entry into the land of Israel is not celebrated in and of itself because, as historic as it was, it is only a means to an end and not an end in itself. It was an opportunity, indeed, the beginning of our opportunity to bring together the Torah and the land. Unfortunately, we were never able to completely exploit this opportunity. The tragedy of Jewish history is that we thrived in the land of Israel – spiritually and materially – for relatively short periods of time. And throughout our long exile, the national life of Israel became dormant and even sickly.[47]

The dangers that challenged generations of Jews still loom large for us – the perception of the land of Israel as merely real estate, divorced from

---

42. Yevamot 71b–72a. Malbim (Yehoshua 5:4) cites the Midrash that the tribe of Levi were always circumcised, as the decree of death in the wilderness did not apply to them.
43. Brachot 48b.
44. Birkat HaMazon.
45. Breisheet 15:18.
46. Malbim, Yehoshua 4:23–24
47. Rav Avraham Yitzchak HaKohen Kook described the religious Jews of the exile as those possessing healthy souls and sick bodies, and the nonreligious Zionists as those possessing healthy bodies and sick souls. The new Jew of the rejuvenated land of Israel, in his formulation, would possess a healthy soul and a healthy body.

Hashem and the Torah, a commodity that can be relinquished or bartered for convenience or the pursuit of worldly illusions. If the land of Israel is not construed as the structure on which the Torah society is built, then it loses its sanctity and essence. This is the corruption that menaced every generation of Jews that dwelled in the land of Israel and is not a problem that first arose in our time.

This corruption was to be averted, or at least minimized, by the method of our entry into the land of Israel: through the splitting of the Jordan River, through the boulders bearing the ideas of Torah that heralded our entry into the land, through the *kohanim* who stood in the river with the *Aron* that caused the water to stand as a column, through the merit of Torah that enabled us to enter and to retain the land, and through the miraculous flight across the Jordan of the *Aron* and the *kohanim*. These informed the people of the unique dimension of the land of Israel – the land that transcends nature – and planted the seeds of the Jewish national life that could have endured forever, and someday will.

That is the task of this and every generation.

Summary

The Jordan River miraculously split in order to underscore to the Jewish people that Hashem was guiding our history, and to dramatize that our longevity in the land of Israel is dependent on the Torah remaining the central focus of our lives.

Chapter Three
YEHOSHUA AND THE ANGEL OF GOD

On the eve of the Jewish people's entry into the land of Israel, Yehoshua revived two defining institutions of Jewish life that surprisingly had been neglected throughout the sojourn in the desert: the rite of circumcision and the *Pesach* offering. "All the people who left [Egypt] were circumcised, but all the people who were born in the wilderness on the way during their exodus from Egypt were not circumcised." An entire generation had perished in the wilderness, "but their children [God] raised in their stead – those Yehoshua circumcised since they were uncircumcised because they did not circumcise them on the way" (Yehoshua 5:5–7). And after celebrating the first anniversary of the redemption from Egypt, the observance of *Pesach* had then been suspended for the duration of the Jewish people's wanderings in the wilderness.

Essentially, Yehoshua repeated the process of redemption that had ushered them out of Egypt exactly forty years earlier. Then, too, the people had been uncircumcised, having forsaken this covenant of Avraham after the death of Yosef.[1] Before the Exodus, Moshe required circumcision of all males – a prerequisite for participation in the *Pesach* offering.[2] "In the merit of the blood of circumcision and the blood of the *Pesach* offering,

---

1. Midrash Shemot Raba 1:8.
2. Shemot 12:48.

[God] redeemed the Jewish people from Egypt, and in their merit we will be redeemed in the future."[3] Maharal[4] comments that *mila* characterizes the Jew as a servant of God on an individual level, and *Pesach* is the prototypical service of God; each is indispensable in creating the Jewish personality who can function as God's agent in the world. These commandments, therefore, are the only two positive commandments – actions – the neglect of which incurs the harsh penalty of *karet*, extinction for the violator.[5] One service binds us to Hashem as individuals, and the other service binds us to Hashem as a nation.

The institutions of *mila* and *Pesach* had to be rejuvenated in order for the people to merit entry into the land of Israel. The nation – and every individual citizen – required re-designation as servants of Hashem entitled to share in His earthly heritage.

There was one further issue with which Yehoshua had to deal before the conquest of the land commenced, and it was raised very subtly during his strange and cryptic encounter with the angel of God.

> And it happened when Yehoshua was in Yericho[6] that he lifted his eyes, and standing opposite him was a man with his sword drawn in his hand. Yehoshua went to him and said to him, "Are you for us or for our enemies?" And he said, "No, I am the commander of the hosts of Hashem, now, I have come."
>
> Yehoshua fell before him to the ground and prostrated himself and said to him, "What does my master say to his servant?" And the commander of Hashem's host said to Yehoshua, "Remove your shoe from your foot, for the place upon which you stand is holy." And Yehoshua did so. (Yehoshua 5:13–15)

There are several unusual facets to this confrontation. Certainly, the obvious question is: Why did this meeting occur at all? What was Yehoshua apprised of, beyond the admonition to remove his shoes? And for what purpose? And for how long? As suddenly as this event occurred, it ended even more abruptly: "And Yehoshua did so." But what was the point of this entire episode?

3. Pirkei D'Rabbi Eliezer, Chapter 29. (Warsaw Edition) See Rashi on Yechezkel 16:6.
4. Gur Aryeh on Shemot 12:6.
5. Mishna Kreitot 1:1.
6. Rashi (Yehoshua 5:13) points out that, obviously, Yehoshua was not inside the city of Yericho but on its outskirts.

The Gemara (Eruvin 63b) states that Yehoshua was admonished by the angel for two sins. "[The angel said to Yehoshua] 'last night you neglected to bring the standard evening offering[7] and now you are neglecting the study of Torah.' 'For which sin have you come?', Yehoshua asked. And the angel answered, 'Now I have come' (for the sin of neglecting Torah study). Immediately, 'Yehoshua went that night into the valley,' (Yehoshua 8:13), i.e., he engaged in the study of the profundities of *halacha*." He resumed his study of Torah, and the angel was assuaged.

The simple understanding of the text would imply that Yehoshua was censured for disregarding his obligation of Torah study during his preparations for war. For sure, the issue of the participation of Torah scholars in national defense is a most vexing one in Israeli society. The Talmud (Bava Batra 7b) makes clear that "the Rabbis do not need the protection [of a wall]" and need not contribute financially to civil defense. Indeed, Avraham himself was punished "because he impressed scholars into military service" (Nedarim 32a).[8] The Torah itself protects forever.[9]

Nevertheless, it is difficult to posit that in every area of life (business, medicine, etc.) – except for personal safety and security – the Torah obligates a person to exert himself to achieve his goals and not rely solely on the intervention of Heaven. For example, a sick person is obligated to seek medical attention, and normative Jewish law prohibits one from passively relying on God's salvation to restore him to good health.[10] A person is similarly obligated to find gainful employment, and not become a public charge or depend on charity for his sustenance. "Everything is in the hands of Heaven" – and yet, we are required to use our wisdom, abilities and resources to live in and develop this world.[11]

Furthermore, Radak rejected the Gemara's interpretation of Yehoshua's sin as stemming from neglect of Torah study, terming it a "far-fetched exposition"[12] and boldly asserting that "wartime is not a time for Torah

---

7. The *korban tamid shel bein ha'arbayim*.
8. Breisheet 14:14. Avraham took the 318 disciples he had educated in his home to wage war with him against the four kings who had captured Avraham's nephew Lot.
9. Sotah 21a.
10. Rambam, Mishna Pesachim 4:9; Responsa *Tzitz Eliezer* XI, Chapter 41.
11. *Chovot HaLevavot* (Duties of the Heart), Rabbenu Bachye, Sha'ar HaBitachon (The Gate of Trust), Chapter 4.
12. "*V'zeh hadrash rachok*" (Radak, Yehoshua 5:14).

study."[13] Many giants of Jewish life – Avraham, Moshe, and especially King David – all went to war, and the Messiah himself is defined as one "who fights God's battles."[14] This conundrum is unresolved; certainly, Talmud Torah is the most important *mitzva* and shapes our performance of all the *mitzvot*,[15] but by the same token the preservation of life takes precedence over all *mitzvot*.[16] Whether or not today's wars in Israel are classified as *milchamot mitzva* (mandatory wars) that would demand the service of all able-bodied individuals[17] is itself part of the discussion. Yehoshua first confronted this unresolved dispute, which rages in modern Israel until today: What is the proper balance between our religious obligations and the practical need to wage wars of conquest or defense?

If we accept the Gemara's position, then Yehoshua here was reminded that the Torah cannot be sacrificed – either its study or the performance of any of its commandments – even for the conquest of the land of Israel. Such conquest is itself a *mitzva*,[18] and presupposes that the *mitzvot* of the Torah will be obeyed. Our possession of the land is premised on our proper observance of the commandments; "if you will follow My decrees and observe My commandments and perform them...you will dwell securely in your land. I will provide peace in the land, and you will lie down with none to frighten you" (Vayikra 26:3, 5–6).

The Jewish soldier does not abandon the Torah when he goes into battle; on the contrary, he is accompanied by a priest anointed especially for this purpose who exhorts the army on the ethics and the philosophical mindset expected of the army of Israel. "And he will say to them, 'Hear O Israel, you are drawing near to the battle against your enemies'" (Devarim 20:3). Rashi comments there that "even if the only merit you have is the recitation of *Shema*, that suffices to evoke God's salvation." In battle, the Jewish soldier must be aware that he is fighting God's battles, and that must be apparent in his motivation, commitment and certainly his ethical

---

13. "*Ein sha'at hamilchama sha'at Talmud Torah*" (ibid.).
14. Rambam, *Laws of Kings and their Wars*, 11:4.
15. Mishna Pe'ah 1:1.
16. Yoma 82a, except for the three cardinal sins of idolatry, homicide and sexual immorality.
17. Sotah 44b.
18. Ramban, on Rambam's *Sefer HaMitzvot*, Mitzvot Aseh omitted by Rambam, 4.

comportment. Thus, warfare is not the province of the morally challenged, but is properly the function of the righteous who are without sin.[19]

This was the final quandary faced by Yehoshua as the battle for Yericho loomed: What would be the effect on the Jewish soul – and psyche – of warfare, violence and brutality? Aggression unleashed in battle is not easily held in check when the soldier returns to civilian life, and can often dominate the soldier's personality and affect all his relationships. In war, problems are solved with violence; in life, violence is destructive. How can the "kingdom of priests and holy nation" remain priestly and holy when wars and weapons are required to protect the Torah's interests?

This was the implication of Yehoshua's prophetic vision.[20] "Behold, a man was standing opposite him with his sword drawn in his hand. Yehoshua went to him and said, 'Are you for us or for our enemies?'" The sword is a powerful weapon, but it can literally be double-edged. In the wilderness where God miraculously provided all the people's needs, there was no danger of being corrupted by the effects of the sword. Similarly, in exile, when Jews were not responsible for their own defense (and frequently paid a heavy price for that), we developed an aversion to violence of any kind. Jews for centuries have been world leaders in most movements advocating pacifism, nonviolence and conciliation. Often deprived of the right of self-defense, Jews made abhorrence of aggression into a virtue. In modern Israel, however, pacifism is not a viable option, as a ruthless enemy is ready, willing and able to exploit peacefulness as a sign of weakness.

The "drawn sword" can be a blessing or a curse, depending on how it is used. For sure, war represents human failure and degradation, a release of man's darkest passions. But war also is perceived as a means of perfecting the world, as the beginning of redemption,[21] and can awaken the power of the Messiah.[22] This was Yehoshua's latent fear: how would combat change the Jewish soldier?[23] Would the sword be *"for us"* – a necessary weapon

19. Rashi (Devarim 20:8) cites Rabbi Yossi Haglili's opinion in Sotah 44a that the soldier who returns home because he is "fearful and fainthearted" is frightened because he is a sinner. By implication, the Jewish army consists of righteous people and scholars.
20. Heard from Rav Yisrael Chait. Note that Rambam (Hilchot Yesodei HaTorah 7:6 and Moreh Nevuchim, Part 2, Chapters 41–43) states that the Tanach frequently employs an "angel" as the means through which a prophetic vision is conveyed.
21. "War is also *atchalta d'geula*, the beginning of redemption" (Megila 17b).
22. Rav Avraham Yitzchak HaKohen Kook, in *Orot*, The War, Chapter 1.
23. This is true notwithstanding that the battle of Yericho did not require Jewish arms,

consecrated for use – or *"for our enemies"* – an uncontrollable force that leaves society vulnerable and terrified?

In Yehoshua's vision, the "angel" answers him that this problem – like most in life – will be resolved by the free choice of the people. "And he said, 'No, I am the commander of the hosts of Hashem, now, I have come.'" *Now, I have come*, to rebuke you for your neglect of Torah study. If your use of weapons and war is always guided and limited by the dictates of the Torah, then you will be successful in battle and remain decent and principled in life. But if you neglect the Torah, give free rein to your basest emotions and instincts, and use your armaments in an unrestrained, undisciplined and immoral way – then eventually those arms will be used inappropriately, corrode your ethical core, and even be turned against your own people.

Israel's modern army has always placed great importance on the concept of "purity of arms," but because those guidelines often conflict with the Torah's precepts, Israel's soldiers are forced to absorb unnecessary casualties[24] and the concept itself – however noble and gallant in theory – is less constructive in practice. It is missing, at least partly, one ingredient.

"And the commander of Hashem's host said to Yehoshua, 'Remove your shoe from your foot, for the place upon which you stand is holy.'" Israel is God's army, Rashi says.[25] One who fights wars and is mindful of the presence of God even on the battlefield is careful to keep his "camp sanctified" (Devarim 23:15) and his personal life pure and chaste. He also recognizes that the place for which he wages war is holy, and therefore the war he fights is not for territory but for holiness itself. Territory is a commodity that can be traded, exchanged or surrendered – like any real estate or other material asset. But sanctity cannot be subject to barter or commerce, for sanctity emerges from a different dimension of existence. If "the place on which you stand is holy," then a different approach to warfare

and that the wars of conquest were designed to succeed with divine assistance and a minimum of Jewish military participation. This dilemma would arise in due time and have a dramatic impact on Jewish society.
24. Witness the heavy death toll incurred by Israel in house-to-house fighting in Jenin and Shechem in 2002, when prudence – and conventional military practice elsewhere – would have called for aerial bombing of the terrorist hideouts. The bitter irony was, of course, that Israel's best (and mostly successful) efforts to avoid Arab civilian casualties failed to prevent the international community from accusing Israel of a civilian massacre – that never took place.
25. Rashi, Yehoshua 5:15.

and settlement is expected; it is a different land that you are about to enter, and your attachment to that land must transcend the purely material or nationalistic attachments that man generally has for his homeland.

This prophetic vision challenged Yehoshua to reiterate his – and his nation's – readiness to embrace this new destiny, with its unique parameters for national life. Could he successfully integrate the ethics of Torah into the practice of war? Could he recognize and impart to his people the uniqueness of the land they were about to conquer and inherit?

In his vision, Yehoshua was asked to remove his shoes in acknowledgment of the sanctity of the land and his acceptance of the criteria of conquest. The same request had been made of his mentor Moshe during his encounter with Hashem at the burning bush, at the very beginning of his mission (Shemot 3:5). Moshe, too, had to see beyond the mundane and humbly embrace the task of consecrating Hashem's world. "And Yehoshua did so… And Hashem was with Yehoshua, and his renown traversed the land" (Yehoshua 5:15, 6:2).

The people, duly circumcised and rejuvenated by their first *Pesach* in the land of Israel, were spiritually prepared. Yehoshua was charged, imbued with a deeper sense of his mission, and the mission of Israel. The conquest of Yericho was at hand.

Summary

Before beginning the conquest of the land, the Jewish people had to replicate the process of redemption in Egypt by again embracing the *mitzvot* of *mila* and *Pesach*. And Yehoshua had to reckon with the proper balance between study of Torah and the conduct of war, and the long-term effects on a pious nation of the culture of violence that war often spawns.

~ Chapter Four
CONQUEST OF YERICHO

Yericho has three major distinctions. It is the lowest city on earth (some nine hundred feet below sea level), the oldest city on earth (with a recorded history of more than four thousand years), and the first Jewish conquest in the land of Israel.[1] The story of its conquest is one of the most famous in the Bible, as conventional military strategy with an army and weapons were spurned. Yericho was vanquished through spiritual weapons alone. The *kohanim* (priests) circled the walls of Yericho while sounding the *shofar* once a day for six days, and then seven times on the seventh day – and the walls came tumbling down.

The story, however, is profound, and its message to Jews resonates until today. Yericho was a unique city that was frequently referred to by our Sages in esoteric ways. For example, notwithstanding that Yericho is located on the northern shore of the Dead Sea, twenty miles east of Yerushalayim, the Gemara Tamid (30b) states that "in Yericho, they were able to *hear* the sound of the opening of the large gate of the Temple Mount, the sound of the *magrefa*,[2] the song of the *Levi'im*, Ben Arza (a Levi) playing the cymbals, the flute, the voice of *Gabini* the herald summoning the *kohanim* and *Levi'im* to the Temple service… and some say even the *kohen gadol's* pronunciation of the ineffable Name of God on Yom Kippur." All this was

---

1. Paradoxically, and not at all unrelated, it was the first city lost by the modern State of Israel to the Palestinian Authority when it was surrendered in 1994.
2. Either a shovel or one of the musical instruments used in the Temple.

heard in Yericho! How is that possible? Apparently, the city of Yericho is intrinsically linked to the divine service in the *Bet HaMikdash*, and to Yerushalayim itself. What is that connection?

Additionally, the Midrash[3] notes that on Succot in the Temple, the people carried their *lulavim* and *etrogim* and circled the altar once a day for six days, and seven times on *Hoshana Raba*. Why? "Rabbi Chiya stated that it was in remembrance of [the events at] Yericho," and this practice is maintained today notwithstanding that there is no Temple or altar. But what is the connection between the *hakafot* (circuits) on *Hoshana Raba* and the battle of Yericho?

Furthermore, Gemara Brachot (54a) comments that one who sees the walls of Yericho which were swallowed up by the ground must recite the blessing of thanksgiving.[4] What is so special about Yericho and this battle?

Elsewhere the Midrash[5] affirms that "when the Jews came to wage war against Yericho, all seven Canaanite nations gathered in Yericho to resist the attack… Did then all seven nations possess Yericho? Rabbi Shmuel bar Nachmani said: 'Yericho is the bolt,[6] the latch, or the door to the vault, of the land of Israel. If Yericho would be conquered, the land entirely would in short order fall to Israel as well.' Therefore, all seven nations gathered in Yericho to fight." Why was this battle the definitive battle for the land of Israel?

In the ancient world, the city of Yericho enjoyed a reputation for impregnability. "And Yericho was completely sealed before the children of Israel; no one left and no one came" (Yehoshua 6:1).[7] It was walled, locked, and fortified. Even its own people, on the eve of war, were prohibited from entering or exiting. Moreover, the walls of the city protected it from invasion, and protected the land as well. Yericho lies in the plains of the

---

3. Yalkut Shimoni, Tehillim, 703.
4. Ruins of these walls are visible today in the ancient city of Yericho, requiring the visitor to recite the blessing "…*she'asa nisim la'avotenu bamakom hazeh*," blessing God Who performed miracles for our fathers in this place. Incidentally, this blessing is also recited by one who sees the place where the Jordan River split and the Jewish people crossed into the land of Israel (Shulchan Aruch, Orach Chaim 218:1).
5. Bamidbar Raba 15:15.
6. The Hebrew word is *nagra*.
7. The Hebrew term is *sogeret u'mesugeret*, literally "closed and closed again." It was closed generally, and further sealed to prevent Israel's entry (Malbim).

Jordan Valley and controls the entrance to the land of Israel. If the city of Yericho is breached and conquered, the invader can then easily ascend the mountains of the Judean desert and have complete access to the land. So Yericho was literally the portal to the land of Israel, and therefore its vital strategic location demanded the strictest security measures. So how could this city be captured?

> God said to Yehoshua, Behold, I have delivered into your hands Yericho and its kings and mighty warriors. You shall circumnavigate the city, all the soldiers encircling the city one time. This should be done for six days. And seven *kohanim* shall carry seven *shofarot* before the Ark, and on the seventh day you shall encircle the city seven times, and the *kohanim* shall blow the *shofarot*. And it shall be that with an extended blast of the shofar – when you hear the sound of the shofar – all the people will cry out with a great cry, and the wall of the city will fall down in its place, and the people shall advance, each man straight ahead. (Yehoshua 6:2–5)

This was the order of battle. The soldiers surrounded the city, followed by the *kohanim* with the *shofarot* and other *kohanim* carrying the Ark of the Covenant, followed by the rear guard of soldiers and the rest of the people. But why were the soldiers needed altogether? They were not fighting, as this was not a conventional war but a war of miracles and Divine Providence. The participation of just the *kohanim* should have sufficed. So why were the soldiers enlisted – and to do little but "pass before the Ark" (6:7), encircle the city and nothing else?

And so it was. For six days, the troops passed before and behind the Ark, surrounded the city, and seven *kohanim* each blew a *shofar*.

> On the seventh day, they arose early at dawn and walked around the city seven times… and on the seventh time the *kohanim* blew the *shofar*. And Yehoshua said to the people, Cry out, for God has given you the city. Everything in the city is consecrated property to God, everyone is to be killed, except for Rachav and her family… The people cried out, the *kohanim* blew the *shofarot*… the wall fell in its place, and the people went up into the city and conquered it… (Yehoshua 6:15–20)

Rachav was saved, the city was utterly destroyed – burnt down – and the material wealth was duly consecrated to God. And the city itself was cursed: "Yehoshua adjured the nation, saying, Cursed before God is the one who arises and rebuilds this city, Yericho; with his oldest child he will lay its foundation and with his youngest he will position its gates" (6:26), meaning that the builder's children will not survive its construction.[8]

A few more questions arise. Why are *shofarot* – usually instruments of prayer – here employed as the weapons of this war? Secondly, the Yerushalmi[9] teaches that a siege of a city cannot be started within three days of the onset of Shabbat, so as not to necessitate undue Shabbat desecration. But this applies only to an optional war. An obligatory war can be waged even on Shabbat, "as we find the conquest of Yericho occurred on Shabbat, as it says, 'do this for six days, and on the seventh day circle the city seven times.'" The *seventh day* was Shabbat, the day on which the walls of Yericho would fall. But why did the conquest have to occur on Shabbat? Why not wait until Sunday? Finally, why did Yehoshua order that the city of Yericho never be rebuilt? In fact, we see that Yericho was repopulated over the ages, including a significant community in Talmudic times.[10] Why was there even a demand that Yericho never be rebuilt? Indeed, the Gemara Sanhedrin (113a) rules that "the name Yericho cannot be applied to another city, nor can another city be built and use the name Yericho"! Why is that?[11]

Approaches

Rav Eliyahu Dessler[12] explained that the essence of *bitachon* (faith in God) is the recognition that everything comes from God. *Emunah* (loosely translated as "belief") is the corpus of philosophical ideas about God and existence that each person possesses, whereas *bitachon* is the effect those ideas have on a person's soul or personality. The framework of *bitachon* is the realization that everything that occurs in life comes from God, and

---

8. This indeed happened centuries later during the reign of the wicked King Achav, when Chiel of Bet El attempted to rebuild Yericho in defiance of the ban (I Melachim 16:34).
9. Yerushalmi Shabbat, Perek 1, page 7b.
10. The "Shalom al Yisrael" synagogue in Yericho dates from the fourth century CE, and stood until ransacked by Arabs after Yericho was surrendered to Arab control in the mid-1990s.
11. A related question, why Yehoshua pronounced a *cherem*, prohibition, on the spoils of Yericho – and only Yericho, of all the cities conquered in the land of Israel – will be discussed in Chapter 5, the "Sin of Achan," who violated that prohibition.
12. *Michtav Me'Eliyahu*, vol. 2, page 262.

man's surrender to that overpowering reality defines his relationship with God. Even though we are obligated to make our own *hishtadlut* (efforts), ultimate success or failure is not dependent on our own exertions but on God's will.

We often think that our actions are the true causes of whatever effects we produce, but, in fact, the ultimate results are reflections of God's will. The only person who need not make any effort is the one who dedicates his entire essence to God and Torah,[13] and this person need not worry about material matters at all. Most people are not on this exalted level, and they are tested by having to "work" for their attainments while still realizing that they are not the ultimate determinants of their success, prosperity or accomplishments. "Many designs are in man's heart, but the counsel of God – only it will prevail" (Mishlei 19:21).

This concept of *bitachon*, so essential for Jewish life at all times, required special enunciation when the conquest of the land of Israel began. This is why Yericho was conquered miraculously – but with the passive involvement of the soldiers who merely circled the city without their traditional weapons. The army of Israel, particularly, needed to be reminded of this basic truth of Jewish history. The Jewish people do not conquer the land of Israel, nor retain the land of Israel, through force of arms and the superiority of our soldiers. "Some with chariots and some with horses – but we, in the Name of God, we call out" (Tehillim 20:8). The irony of modern Jewish life in Israel is that when the Israel Defense Forces were perceived as outmanned and outgunned, the underdogs and the weaker party – e.g., the War of Independence, the Six-Day War, the Yom Kippur War – the IDF was successful and victorious (not to mention Israel was slightly more popular internationally). In recent years, though, as Israel is perceived as the superior military force, the most powerful army in the Middle East, it cannot vanquish its foes, is weaker and more vulnerable than before, and has gradually lost its will to fight and defend its homeland. That is because the land of Israel is neither conquered nor retained through physical might alone.

This was the lesson taught by the assault on Yericho – and the invasion

---

13. See Rambam, *Hilchot Shmita v'Yovel*, 13:12–13, where Rambam thus characterizes the tribe of Levi as a whole, along with all others who aspire to this life of complete and faithful dependence on God.

of the land of Israel generally. The people were promised that, if they were worthy, they would defeat the kings of Canaan and capture the land without even one casualty, an impossibility in warfare; hence, the mortification (and admission of sin) when thirty-six Jewish soldiers were killed in the battle of Ai.[14] Yericho established the basic principle of conquest – and even our elementary military maneuvers there were pointless. After Yericho, our *hishtadlut* is required, but we do not rely on or expect our own power to provide either partial or total victory. Our efforts reflect our desire not to depend on miracles, and to accept humbly the Providential nature of our existence. We never believe for a moment that our success or failure hinges on anything but our spiritual standing before God, and His will.

That is why it was crucial to preserve the memory of this miracle in a number of ways – especially, as the Yalkut Shimoni cited above notes, through the *hakafot* on *Succot* and *Hoshana Raba*. Rav Yitzchak ibn Gias,[15] based on the Yerushalmi, explained that we commemorate the conquest of Yericho on *Hoshana Raba*. *Succot* itself is a celebration of the land of Israel and the miracles that occurred there.[16] The first miracle in the land itself, and the miracle that created the framework for our possession of the land, was the capture of Yericho. The Rambam adds that this is why Yehoshua decreed that Yericho never be rebuilt, so that it should remain an eternal wonder, a spectacle to onlookers. "Whoever sees the walls of Yericho sunk in the ground will recognize that this was no ordinary destruction, but rather that the city walls collapsed miraculously."[17]

Indeed, Chazal aver that the walls of Yericho did not come tumbling down, but rather were absorbed into the ground. "Since their thickness and height were identical, it had to sink into the ground" (Berachot 54b), or, as Rashi adds, the wall's collapse would not have been noticeable. Sunken walls, covered by layers of subsequent civilizations, still remain, as eloquent testimony to the miracle and the supremacy of God's will.

Rav Dessler further elucidated that the "great cry" of the people (Yehoshua 6:20) demonstrated to them the futility of human endeavors in comparison to God's will. "…If God will not guard the city, in vain is

---

14. See below Chapter 5, "The Sin of Achan" (Yehoshua, Chapter 7).
15. *Hilchot Ritz Gias*, vol. 1, Lulav, page 114; Maharasha on Succa 45a; based on Yerushalmi Succa 4:3.
16. Rambam, *Moreh Nevuchim*, Part 3, Chapter 43, in reference to the Four Species.
17. Ibid., Part 3, Chapter 50.

the watchman vigilant" (Tehillim 127:1). Nor should one be concerned, as Ralbag feared, that this miracle left skeptics with a possible "natural" explanation of events – that the excessive noise brought the walls down. Skeptics will try to dismiss every miracle as naturalistic, a coincidence, or predictable – and this option is allowed them in order to maintain their right of free choice. Even miracles test our faith – our faith that God's hand does control all.

The settlement of the land of Israel is dependent on a renunciation of the illusion that "my strength and the might of my hand produced for me all this wealth" (Devarim 8:17). This attitude is the kernel of heresy and disbelief, and the rejection of this idea is the guarantee of our permanent residence in the land. Thus, once Yericho was conquered, immediately the entire land could be conquered;[18] i.e., once we established and embraced the principle that warriors do not overpower the nations of Canaan but the will of God does, then the entire land of Israel was easily subjugated. Yericho was the *nagra*, the deadbolt, of the land of Israel,[19] not because of the city itself but because of the nature of the conquest and what it symbolized. "And God was with Yehoshua, and his renown spread throughout the land" (6:27). The thirty-one kings of Canaan began to flee in panic, as they could not resist this most unconventional adversary.

This is also why we are obligated to recite the blessing of thanksgiving when we view the walls of Yericho. In fact, Chazal state that Yehoshua composed *Aleinu*, the famous prayer of gratitude that concludes each of our prayer services, during the seven days of circling Yericho.[20] To "thank Hashem" is to recognize His hand in all our affairs, and sublimate our will to His will. Our rights to the land of Israel are reinforced by this acknowledgment, and undermined by its repudiation.

How were all the sounds from the *Bet HaMikdash* (the gates opening, the song of the *Levi'im*, the call of the *shofar*, etc.) "heard" in Yericho?[21] Chazal perceived Yericho's status as analogous to that of Yerushalayim, because it was the very beginning of the conquest of the land of Israel. Yericho was the first place where the holy people encountered the holy land, where the sanctity of the Jewish people became linked with the sanctity

---

18. Bamidbar Raba 15:15.
19. Ibid.
20. *Kol Bo*, Chapter 16, cited in Mishbetzot Zahav, page 117.
21. Masechet Tamid 30b.

of the land of the Jews. The holiest place in Israel is the Holy of Holies in Yerushalayim – but Yericho was the place where the people who are the natural possessors of the land of Israel first enjoyed the holiness of the land of Israel. So Yericho always *echoed* the sounds of Yerushalayim; there, in Yericho, we first experienced the *kedushat Eretz Yisrael* (the sanctity of the land) that would only culminate with the conquest of Yerushalayim in David's time.[22]

The miraculous crossing of the Jordan enunciated the idea that all nature is in God's hands, but that idea blossomed and achieved fruition at the first act of conquest, in Yericho. The soldiers were placed front and center to impress upon them – and the nation – that soldiers do not win battles or wars. A different force – the hand of Hashem – fights for the Jewish people.

Return to Nature

The miracle accomplished something else as well.[23] The seven days of the "battle" of Yericho paralleled the seven days of creation, and the people were introduced to a unique aspect of Divine Providence. Just as Shabbat does not nullify the laws of nature but consecrates them, so too the miracle at Yericho did not tamper with or destroy nature but restored it to its pristine state. Walls are human devices; walls do not exist in nature. Walls are man's attempt to project strength, invincibility and eternity,[24] a symbol of man's ego and bluster.

These walls, emblematic of ancient man's illusion of his own indomitable might, receded into the ground, and returned the land of Israel to

---

22. Similarly, the *kohen* in charge of beginning the daily service in the Temple would ask each morning: "Is the eastern sky lit? Until Hevron?" (Yoma 28a). This daily directive reinforced the centrality of the *Avot*, our forefathers, the "slumberers of Hevron," to our rights to the land of Israel, and reminded the people of the divine promise to the *Avot* through which we conquered and possessed the land. In this way, each city bore an intrinsic connection to Yerushalayim, which was – and is – the spiritual center of Jewish life. This connection was underscored, in each case, through different aspects of the *avoda* in the Temple.
23. *Me'avoor Ha'aretz*, page 69.
24. Like the Great Wall of China, the only man-made entity visible from space. (World Book Encyclopedia of Science: The Planet Earth, page 15, Chicago, 1990). Nevertheless, many people assert that the Great Wall's visibility from space is a popular myth; if so, the myth endures because it reinforces the fantasy of man's immense power and invincibility.

its natural state – a state of nature, utterly dependent on God for its sustenance and preservation. Thus, *only* Yericho could not be rebuilt, because the first conquest of part of the land of Israel had to always remain in its natural, unadorned, unembellished state, a testament to the *Yad Hashem* and an eternal reminder that Yericho was the portal to the land of Israel.[25] The land of Israel demands that we harmonize human endeavor with the divine will, in a way that does not exist in any other land.[26] This surrender to God is illustrated in Zechariah's prophecy that at the end of days "*Prazot teshev Yerushalayim*," Yerushalayim will be settled beyond its walls (Zechariah 2:8), an open expanse, unafraid of invaders or marauders. Its wall will be the divine "wall of fire all around, and for glory will I be in its midst" (Zecharia 2:9).[27] The disappearance of the walls of Yericho was a foretaste of that glorious future.

The miracle at Yericho essentially took this magnificent example of human power and ingenuity – the unconquerable walls – and humbled it, demonstrating its impotence before Hashem. That is why the *shofar* was used, and not the trumpets ordinarily blown during battle.[28] Trumpets are man-made instruments; *shofarot* are natural instruments. Ordinary wars require the use of trumpets, fashioned by man out of metal and reflecting his compulsory involvement. Here, nature – the power of the Creator – was the means of conquest, and so the weapon of war was the natural *shofar*, a detached but unimproved part of an animal.[29] Here, the vehicle of conquest was God's mastery, not human mastery.

We relate the physical world to the Creator in two ways. One way is by infusing nature with *mitzvot*. Every aspect of nature can be sanctified

---

25. Once Yericho was unlawfully rebuilt by Chiel, Yehoshua's prohibition lapsed and Jews subsequently lived there for centuries (*Meshech Chochma*). This, too, likely reflects the Jews' insensitivity – and unwillingness – to leaving Yericho in its pristine state as evidence of the hand of God.
26. *Mitzvot* are our means of sanctifying nature, of subordinating our will to that of Hashem. In terms of a land, though, which exists to reflect God's will, the land of Israel is unique. "A land that God seeks out; the eyes of God are always upon it, from the beginning of the year to year's end" (Devarim 11:12).
27. Yerushalayim will extend all the way to Damascus. Contrast this with today's unfortunate situation in which Israel's Jews live behind walls and fences, while the Arabs roam free and unfettered.
28. Bamidbar 10:1–10.
29. *Me'avoor Ha'aretz*, pages 69–70, quoting Rav Avraham Yitzchak HaKohen Kook.

to God's service at some point: our bodies, foods, buildings, clothing, etc. All have particular *mitzvot* that link these entities – and the performers of these *mitzvot* – to Hashem. The second way is through developing nature ourselves. Here, the *shofar* is the natural vessel elevated in its purposes to carry out a lofty mission. Indeed, just as on Rosh Hashana we minimize human achievement and use the natural *shofar* in our prayers, so too the very first battle for the land of Israel demanded that we defer to God, minimize human achievement and utilize this natural implement. That is why on Rosh Hashana we recite Tehillim 47[30] a total of seven times before *shofar*-blowing – in commemoration of the conquest of Yericho that occurred after it was encircled seven times by seven *kohanim* with seven *shofarot*. Both events suggest human submissiveness before God.[31]

Rav Dessler explained the use of the *shofarot* here in a different, more profound manner. The *shofar* is the instrument of *teshuva*, repentance – and repentance is the secret weapon of the army of Israel. Before entering battle, the soldiers would be admonished to repent,[32] and through Yehuda HaMaccabi's time, the Jewish army always fasted on the day of battle. Israel's wars aim to uproot impurity from the land, and this can only be achieved if our own spirits are pure. That is why Israel conquered Yericho through *hakafot*, surrounding and encircling the city. The impurity of Yericho was surrounded by holiness, bottled up and then nullified. When the foundations of *tumah* were deracinated, then Yericho's walls simply collapsed – and that was the conquest of Yericho. The *shofar*, the tool of repentance, was instrumental in severing the spiritual pollution implanted in the land of Israel by the seven Canaanite peoples.[33]

There are three forms of holiness in the world: the Jewish people among mankind, Shabbat in time, and the land of Israel in space. The subjugation of Yericho signified an explosion of holiness into the world. This first conquest required that the paradigms of *kedusha* (holiness) all be utilized – in effect, that there would be a maximization of holiness.

---

30. "For Hashem is supreme, awesome; a great King over the earth. He shall lead nations under us and regimes beneath our feet. He will choose our heritage for us… Hashem reigns over the nations…" (Tehillim 47:3–5, 9).
31. *Mishbetzot Zahav*, page 113.
32. This was the intent of the declaration to those who are "fearful and fainthearted" (Devarim 20:8, and Rashi's commentary thereon).
33. *Michtav Me'Eliyahu*, vol. 2, pages 264–265.

Therefore, the holy people had to conquer the holy land, and on the holiest day, Shabbat.[34] The *kohanim* are the holiest class of Jews, and they blew the *shofarot* and brought the walls down. It was a cataclysmic eruption of *kedusha* and set the tone for our possession of the land.[35]

The conquest of Yericho was exceptional because it connected the holy people to the holy land, and taught us that the settlement of the land was dependent on Hashem and not on armies or weapons. It was the ultimate denial – and a constant reminder – of the illusion implicit in "my power and the might of my hand brought me this wealth." But even this lesson would soon be lost, and that illusion would appear and haunt generation after generation – beginning immediately with the sin of Achan.

Because Yericho was captured utilizing the three *kedushot*, it was the springboard (and later, the echo) of Yerushalayim, the holy city. The spirit of Yericho heralded the conquest of the land, even as in recent years it has symbolized Israel's retreat from the land itself. First Yericho was surrendered, then the city of Shechem (where Avraham first set foot in the land),[36] then the city of our fathers, Hevron. Even if those cities have partially returned to Jewish control, the unequivocal and unambiguous assertion of Jewish rights to those cities has not yet followed. And those cities form a triangle around Yerushalayim, the heart of the land of Israel and the symbol of our national presence.

To regain and hold onto the land of Israel, we need an injection of the spirit of Yericho – of acceptance of our destiny and surrender to Hashem's guiding hand – and the aura that arose from its conquest and engendered "and God was with Yehoshua and his renown spread throughout the land" (Yehoshua 6:27). When we recover that aura, our adversaries will tremble in awe before us, and *Yishuv Eretz Yisrael* (the settlement of the land) will be secured for our generation and future generations.

---

34. *Mishbetzot Zahav*, page 116, quotes the Yerushalmi Moed Katan (9a) that cites the conquest of Yericho on Shabbat as the source of the *halacha* that one can violate a Rabbinic prohibition (*shevut*) on Shabbat in order to acquire property in the land of Israel and fulfill the *mitzva* of Yishuv Eretz Yisrael.
35. *Me'avoor Ha'aretz*, page 71.
36. Breisheet 12:6.

Summary
The miracle of Yericho is a constant reminder that military prowess is an insignificant factor in the conquest of *Eretz Yisrael*. The fundamental weapons are an awareness of the might of Hashem, surrender to His will, and the infusion of holiness into the land itself.

Chapter Five
THE FIRST SIN:
THE SPOILS OF ACHAN

The sin of Achan was the first sin committed in the land of Israel, and was therefore calamitous, impairing the ability of the Jewish people to fulfill its destiny in the land. The nature and repercussions of Achan's sin are similar to those of the sin of the spies in the wilderness which delayed our entry into Israel for thirty-eight years. Achan's sin was a terrible trauma, jeopardized and desecrated our conquest of the land, and forever changed our relationship with the land of Israel. Its harmful effects sound exaggerated, until we realize the severity with which our Sages perceived this sin.

The question is: How could one man's sin, however notorious, reflect so poorly and permanently on an entire society?

The Torah states that Avraham first entered Israel near Shechem, then headed east, pitching his tent at a mountain, "with Bet El to the west and Ai on the east. And he built an altar to Hashem and called out in Hashem's name" (Breisheet 12:8). Why did Avraham build his first altar there, at Ai? Rashi comments that "he prophesied that his descendants would stumble there because of the sin of Achan, and so Avraham prayed there for them." Of course, this requires elaboration: What does it mean that Avraham prophesied, and prayed for his progeny more than four centuries into the future? In any event, Chazal perceived the enduring harm caused by this sin. What was the sin? And why was it so destructive?

Before conquering Yericho, Yehoshua declared that the property of the city must remain untouched.

> The city and all that is in it shall be consecrated property to God.... Only you, beware of the consecrated property, lest you cause destruction if you take from the cherem (consecrated property) and you bring destruction on the camp of Israel and cause it trouble. All the silver and gold and vessels of copper and iron are holy to God, they shall go to the treasury of God. (Yehoshua 6:17–19)

This directive deviated from the plain law of the Torah, as the Torah had specifically permitted the Jews to enjoy the spoils of their conquests in the land of Israel. "You shall consume the booty of your enemies which God has given you" (Devarim 20:14). Generally, the spoils of war were permitted – but Yericho was the exception. Rashi[1] explains that the property of Yericho was deemed *hekdesh*, consecrated and untouchable, because the conquest of Yericho took place on the holy Shabbat when such mercenary activities are prohibited.

Malbim[2] offers a more philosophical reason. Since the conquest of Yericho was miraculous and did not require any human military initiative, the consecration of the property and its dedication to the Tabernacle was the acknowledgment that God's hand was exclusively responsible for the victory. If the people took spoils, it would indicate that they had somehow participated in the battle and therefore deserved to share in the proceeds of conquest. That would negate the unique message of this first conquest[3] – that the land itself is holy to God and our rights to the land are utterly dependent on our subservience to God. As this was the first conquest, Yehoshua underscored this point by banning the spoils of Yericho – but only Yericho. The first act of conquest had to be completely holy, and the property consecrated to God.

Nevertheless, "the children of Israel trespassed against the consecrated property; Achan son of Carmi, son of Zabdi, son of Zerach, from the tribe of Yehuda, took of the consecrated property, and the anger of God flared against the Children of Israel" (Yehoshua 7:1).

It would not be long before the sin – *of one person* – was exposed.

---

1. Yehoshua 6:17.
2. Ibid.
3. See above, Chapter 4, "The Conquest of Yericho."

Yehoshua sent his trusted spies (Pinchas and Calev) to scout the city of Ai, and they returned with promising intelligence. "The entire people need not go up; about two or three thousand men should go up and smite Ai. Do not weary the entire nation there, because they are few" (Yehoshua 7:3). Ai was defended by a militarily weak and numerically small garrison. Yehoshua sent three thousand soldiers who attacked Ai, with tragic and shocking results. "They fled before the men of Ai, and the men of Ai struck down *about thirty-six* of them" (Yehoshua 7:4–5), the first – and only – casualties they suffered in the wars of conquest. The men of Ai then pursued the soldiers of Israel down the mountain, and drove them away ignominiously.

This was an unprecedented debacle. The Jews had enjoyed the divine promise that God would do the fighting, and the people would conquer the land of Israel without suffering any losses. The conquest of Yericho proceeded smoothly, but as soon as the people actually fought a battle themselves, they were routed by the enemy and failed to achieve their objective. The nation was stunned. "And Yehoshua tore his garments and fell on his face to the ground before the Ark of Hashem until evening,[4] he and the elders of Israel; and they placed dirt upon their heads" (7:6).

Yehoshua, perplexed, asked God in an almost accusatory manner:[5]

> Why did you bring the people across the Jordan to deliver us into the hands of the Emori, to destroy us? If only we had been content to dwell on the other side of the Jordan… All the inhabitants will hear, surround us, and cut off our name from the earth. What will You do for Your Great Name? (Yehoshua 7:7–9).[6]

Why, you ask? The explanation is simple.

> And Hashem said to Yehoshua, Raise yourself up, why do you fall on your face? Israel has sinned, they have also violated My covenant that I commanded them, they have also taken from the consecrated property, they have also stolen, they have also denied it, they have also

---

4. This is one source for the custom of reciting the *Tachanun* prayer (on most weekday mornings and afternoons) while leaning on one's arm if a Sefer Torah is present. See Mishna Berura, Orach Chaim 131:11.
5. An echo of his teacher Moshe, who similarly questioned God at the inauspicious beginning of Moshe's own service to the Jewish people (Shemot 5:22–23).
6. This resembles Moshe's lament after the sin of the golden calf (Shemot 32:11–13) and the sin of the spies (Bamidbar 14:15–17) that the destruction of the Jewish people will constitute a desecration of God's name in the world.

placed it in their vessels… They will not be able to stand before their enemies, they have become worthy of destruction. I will not continue to be in your midst if you do not destroy the transgressor from your midst. (Yehoshua 7:10-12)

But God refused to identify the guilty party to Yehoshua,[7] and suggested that Yehoshua use the *Urim v'Tumim*[8] to expose the person. First the tribe will be revealed, then the family, the household and finally the person himself – and that person should be "burned, he and all his possessions, because he has violated the covenant of Hashem, and because he has committed an abomination in Israel" (7:15).

As God commanded, Yehoshua used the *Urim v'Tumim* to identify the tribe, and then used lots until Achan himself was revealed as the culprit. After Yehoshua's gentle prodding, Achan confessed to taking from Yericho "a fine Babylonian garment, two hundred shekels of silver and one bar of gold" (7:21) and hiding them in the ground within his tent. Curiously, Achan confessed to other sins as well, "indeed, I have sinned against the God of Israel, thus and thus have I done" (7:20). He was taken to the valley of Achor, and, in front of his entire family, summarily executed. "And Yehoshua said, why have you caused us trouble? Hashem will cause you trouble this day. Then all of Israel stoned him, burned them[9] with fire and stoned them"[10] (7:25). And God's anger subsided, and Ai was easily conquered shortly thereafter.

Questions

Why does God introduce Achan's sin by asserting that *"Israel has sinned"*? Actually, only *one person* sinned out of a nation of more than six hundred thousand men and perhaps close to three million people in all. In Moshe's fearful words after the sin of Korach, "shall one man sin, and You be angry with the entire congregation?" (Bamidbar 16:22). We have here a compel-

---

7. In Chazal's phrase (Sanhedrin 43b), God refused to be an "informer," or to speak *lashon hara* against a Jew!
8. The letters on the stones of the breastplate of the *kohen gadol* lit up in response to a request of the king, the Sanhedrin or the high priest himself, and the letters were then prophetically interpreted to convey the divine message. It functioned as a form of prophecy. (Shemot 28:30; Bamidbar 27:21; Yoma 73a–b.)
9. His illicit booty.
10. His stolen animals.

ling and frightening application of collective guilt, as if the Jewish people generally are to be faulted for even one solitary sinner in their midst. Is that just? What lesson is being taught?

Why did Achan sin? What was his motivation? Only the spoils of Yericho were forbidden; if Achan was financially strapped, he only had to wait to the next battle for his big payday. What tempted him? And why does the Navi cite Achan's full genealogy twice (7:17 and 7:24)? Once identified, we know his full – royal – background, a scion of the tribe of Yehuda. So why is this information repeated?

Furthermore, the Gemara (Sanhedrin 43b–44a) derived the obligation of all convicts facing execution to confess their sins ("as all who confess have a share in the world-to-come") from the case of Achan, who was encouraged by Yehoshua to confess. And did he! "Indeed, I have sinned against the God of Israel, thus and thus have I done" (7:20). Achan confessed to three acts of theft – twice during Moshe's time[11] and once now – rendering Achan a persistent felony offender. And Chazal piled a cluster of other, even graver sins on Achan's head: "He violated the five books of the Torah, he tried to conceal his circumcision, and he raped a betrothed woman."[12] Why did Chazal supplement his one sin with many other sins? And why was he executed? If he stole, he should have been forced to return his theft as the Torah ordains (Vayikra 5:23). Rashi[13] explains that he was executed because he violated the Shabbat laws, carrying his loot from a private to a public domain on Shabbat when the conquest of Yericho took place. But the Navi made no explicit reference to this desecration of Shabbat, and in any event, that crime would have required witnesses and testimony to justify his execution. His own confession would have been inadmissible. So why was he executed?

And yet, a profound teaching emerged from Achan's case that shapes Jewish life until today. "And God said to Yehoshua, ...*Israel* has sinned" (Yehoshua 7:10–11). As despicable a sinner as was Achan, he was still re-

---

11. During Moshe's wars against Sichon and the Canaanite tribes. Another opinion states he stole a total of five times, including four during Moshe's wars. Achan was not punished earlier, the Gemara explains, because before the Jews entered the land of Israel, they were not punished for *nistarot*, hidden crimes, but only for crimes that were witnessed and therefore subject to the jurisdiction of a *bet din*.
12. Sanhedrin 44a.
13. Yehoshua 7:25.

ferred to as a Jew: "A Jew who sins is still considered a Jew."[14] No matter how much a Jew strays from Torah – even to the point of renouncing his faith – he still remains a Jew, an explicit refutation to the canard circulated by some non-Orthodox Jews that the Torah world does not consider them Jewish. Even the scoundrel Achan was still a Jew!

The Gemara (Sanhedrin 44a) continues: "'I saw a lovely Babylonian garment,' either silk or dyed wool. The Sanhedrin spread out the cloak before God, and asked plaintively: 'Must thirty-six Jews [killed in the battle of Ai], a majority of the Sanhedrin, die because Achan stole this article of clothing?' Was it worth thirty-six lives?" Chazal hasten to add that, in fact, thirty-six Jews did not die, only one, "Yair ben Menashe, who was equivalent to a numerical majority of the Sanhedrin." Hence, the verse (7:5) specified that "the men of Ai smote *about* thirty-six of the [Jews]." The ambiguity is meant to highlight that only one person was killed. What are Chazal teaching us here? Were thirty-six people killed or only one, and what was the significance if the only victim was Yair the son of Menashe – who was surely quite elderly by this time?

The basic question is: Why did Achan sin? Was it greed, jealousy, heresy or something else? Why did Yehoshua employ the *Urim v'Tumim* to expose the guilty party? And what is the essential lesson of the sin of Achan?

"Israel Has Sinned"
The Book of Yehoshua will never be nullified, even in the time of Moshiach, because the Navi here delineated not only the distribution of the land of Israel, but also the roots of our possession of the land, the framework through which we possess the land, our inalienable right to the land, what enables us to retain the land, and ultimately the seeds of the sinful behavior that would – twice – deprive us of the land for most of our history.

Why were all Jews blamed for Achan's sin – "Israel has sinned" (7:11)? Malbim explained (7:1) that all Jews constitute one body, and all Jews are different limbs of that body. The Mechilta (Shemot 19:5) similarly explicates the Torah's reference to the Jewish people as a "*goy kadosh,*" a holy nation. The word *goy* (as noted above)[15] is derived from the Hebrew word

---
14. Sanhedrin 44a.
15. See Chapter 2, note 40.

gviya, meaning body. A nation is a body, a conglomerate of many different constituent elements. A healthy body has all its limbs and organs, and every Jew is a different limb or organ of the body of Israel. Some Jews are hearts, some are brains, some are arms, legs, toes, knees, shins, hair, nails, etc. – but every Jew is an inherent part of the body. Thus, we mourn the loss of any Jew, as death diminishes the corpus of Israel.

If even one person sins, the Malbim wrote, it has the same effect on the body as if one organ or one limb were impaired. Thus, even though Achan sinned alone, it was as if all Jews somehow shared in his sin and endured its effects.

Furthermore, Malbim commented, there is a difference between an actual punishment from God and the simple removal of Divine Providence. Here, the losses on the battlefield were not a direct punishment, but reflected an act of *hester panim*,[16] a concealment of the divine presence. Hashem suppressed His Providential supervision and abandoned the Jewish people to the natural fate of armies in battle. The people of Ai defended their homeland with honor and valor, they had weapons and will, and inflicted a defeat on the army of Israel. What happened to Yehoshua's army is what can happen to any army – to be routed by a given adversary on a given day, even an adversary that is militarily and numerically inferior. When we are worthy, the prophecy of Yeshayahu (54:17) pertains, that "any weapon sharpened against you will not succeed." When we are unworthy, then the natural laws of warfare prevail and soldiers are killed in battle. Here, at Ai, the Jewish people were not worthy and suffered the consequences.

For sure, collective responsibility is a sibling to collective guilt, which the enemies of Israel down to our day have used to scapegoat entire communities of Jews for the sins of a few. We, in fact, experience this sensation when we read or hear about the misdeeds of an individual Jew, and perceive it as a poor reflection on all of us (a "*shandeh* before the nations"). Is this collective guilt admirable? Why should an individual sin reflect on all Jews?

Rav Avraham Yitzchak HaKohen Kook explained that in the land of Israel, *achdut*, unity, is a literal concept. There, the national soul is alive, and there, our common destiny is felt most intensely (like the unified body in the Malbim's analogy). Only in Israel can real *arevut* take place, the

---

16. Devarim 31:18.

notion that all Jews are responsible and guarantors for one another. That feeling can exist in the exile on some level, but it is experienced in its fullest sense only in the land of Israel. In exile, Jews have a diminished capacity to experience all aspects of Jewish nationhood. In Israel, we as a people have the potential to be whole, and therefore embrace a sense of collective responsibility. As such, when even one Jew sins, Hashem's protective hand can be withdrawn, and we are left to the natural forces that govern relations between states and peoples – with the potential for confrontation and deadly conflict.[17]

The sixteenth-century sage R. Levi ibn Chaviv wrote:

> For all Jews to be gathered together and merit Divine Providence and miraculous intervention requires that every Jew be righteous. If even one Jew sins, then it is as if one limb on the body takes ill. We say not that the limb is ill, but that the person is ill. And we become unworthy of the Divine Providence, and this is also true justice.[18]

Generally, but especially in Israel, the individual persona of the Jew is muted, and is superseded by his share in the national identity. That is why the *Viduy*, the confessional prayers recited on the *Yamim Noraim*, are always phrased in the plural – "for sins *we* committed before You" – we, not I. "We trespassed, we betrayed, we stole, etc." Even if the particular Jew reciting *Viduy* may not have perpetrated that specific sin, invariably some other Jew somewhere did. We do not merely confess our individual sins, but our *Viduy* has to account for the sins of all Jews (especially those who are not confessing them).

This was Achan's fundamental error.[19] A Jew cannot be an individualist who distances himself from the community and locks himself within his own four cubits or *shtiebel*. The Jewish life of every individual Jew has a profound public dimension to it; he is inextricably part of the community of Israel. There are no private Jews, and certainly regarding the land of Israel every Jew is gripped by the holiness of the place and is indispens-

---

17. *Me'avoor Ha'aretz*, page 77–78, citing Rav Avraham Yitzchak HaKohen Kook in *Orot, Orot Yisrael*, 7, 18.
18. Responsa of R. Levi ibn Chaviv (Maharlbach, 77). R. Levi (1485–1545) escaped from Spain and Portugal with his famous father, R. Yaakov ibn Chaviv, author of the Ein Yaakov commentary on the Aggadot of the Talmud. R. Levi became the Chief Rabbi of Yerushalayim in 1524 and a universally acknowledged Torah scholar.
19. *Me'avoor Ha'aretz*, page 84.

ably bound to it. But the most comprehensive expression of the "public" aspect of Jewish life is only found in Israel, and not in the exile. Achan's sin purported to renounce this principle. He professed that a Jew can have an "individual" sin, that what one Jew does need not affect other Jews. That was his fatal mistake – a denial of the collective responsibility that is the essence of our attachment to the land of Israel. Such an approach to Jewish life had to be repudiated by Yehoshua in the most dramatic way.

Rav Dessler[20] underscores this point with a slight variation. It is true that every Jew is a representative of the Jewish people generally, but if Achan sinned, it meant that there was something deficient in the community as a whole – that the environment in which Achan lived was not sufficiently sanctified so as to preclude the possibility of anyone harboring heretical thoughts or illegitimate desires. This, then, is a societal problem, so Hashem challenged Yehoshua: "*Israel* has sinned." An abomination that occurs in the Jewish community is a sign that the community on some level tolerates or condones such acts, or does not bear the requisite horror at its commission. It need not even reach the level of "having the opportunity to protest and not protesting";[21] it can manifest itself as an unwillingness to rebuke the sinner that stems not from misplaced humility[22] but from a liberal notion of tolerance – the American virtue of "live and let live" – or even from sympathy or a vicarious identification with the sinner.

That type of tolerance reflects poorly on the Jewish community and is the "microscopic deficiency" in the moral level of the Jewish community that Rav Dessler laments. There is a limit to the individual autonomy of any Jew, for the community pays the ultimate price for the actions of even one renegade. Achan's sin was our sin.

Achan's Mistake

Achan's name emerged from Yehoshua's lottery as the guilty party, and Achan immediately protested.

> Because of this lottery, I am going to be executed? Achan thought to himself: "Now that I am trapped, I am better off denying the validity of this lottery, so Yehoshua will think I am a liar but all Israel will not

---

20. *Michtav Me'Eliyahu*, vol. 1, page 162.
21. See Masechet Shabbat 55a.
22. Arachin 16b, and Rashi's commentary on "*anava she'lo lishma,*" false modesty.

think me a criminal." Achan said to Yehoshua: "Instead of you drawing lots between me and my family, let me draw lots between you and Pinchas!"[23]

Yehoshua answered calmly, even soothingly, "My son, please give honor to Hashem, and confess to Him. Tell me please what you have done, do not withhold anything from me" (Yehoshua 7:19). But Achan's complaint is seemingly valid and unaddressed by Yehoshua: By the time the lot is limited to a choice between two people, invariably one will be selected. What, then, is the proof of Achan's guilt? How did Yehoshua refute Achan's argument?

Additionally, and ominously, when Achan challenged Yehoshua's authority, the Jewish people suddenly split into warring factions. "The tribe of Yehuda arose and began killing other factions who were contending with them. At that point Achan said to himself: 'Whoever saves one life in Israel it is as if he has saved an entire world. Because of me, Jews are being killed, and I am a sinner and one who causes others to sin. Better that I should confess to Hashem and Yehoshua so this disaster does not come to pass on my account.'" He then confessed fully, completely and voluntarily.[24] What prompted Achan to confess? From where did he generate this concern for the community of Israel?

Achan's contrition and repentance were notable for another reason as well. He admitted taking the garment and the money, and then added to the assembled: "You should not think that I took all this wealth because I was poor; on the contrary, I am the richest member of my tribe."[25] So why did he take it? What dynamic was taking place beneath the surface of these exchanges?

Achan attacked the lottery system and the Divine Providence that suggested it as a masked assault on Yehoshua's authority. This was the first, and very subtle, rebellion against Yehoshua; his master Moshe had been less fortunate, having to ward off a number of serious, palpable threats to his leadership. But Achan based his challenge to Yehoshua on grounds similar

23. Midrash Bamidbar Raba 23:6.
24. Ibid. Rashi (Yehoshua 7:20) says that Achan confessed when he saw that the tribe of Yehuda was preparing for war, but they had neither yet killed anyone nor openly rebelled against Yehoshua. Achan said: "Better I should die alone than that several thousand Jews should die together with me."
25. Midrash Bamidbar Raba 23:6.

to those of Moshe's archrival Korach: It is true that I deny the efficacy of the lottery. More importantly, I have looked into the Torah myself, and we were promised that "everything that will be in the city – all of its booty – may you plunder for yourselves" (Devarim 20:14). So we are inherently allowed to take spoils. You, Yehoshua, are distorting the Torah for your own personal reasons. You are a descendant of Yosef, termed by Yaakov the *nazir echav*, the most abstinent of the brothers (Breisheet 49:26). Who are you to impose your stringencies on all of us? I did not take the spoils because I needed them,[26] but to prove a broader point. Yehoshua is corrupting the Torah, and that is intolerable.[27]

Achan's grievance focused on two different areas and quickly drew supporters (as every malcontent always does). In fact, as noted, the tribe of Yehuda was ready to wage war to uphold these two sacred principles. Yehoshua was challenged as a religious authority, and his usurpation of power as the king (and court) trampled on the rights of the *tribe of Yehuda* as the royal house of Israel. They were content to allow Yehoshua to lead them into the land as Moshe had instructed, but they were not ready to abdicate their royal prerogatives and permit Yehoshua to rule as a monarch – even summarily executing one of their own tribesmen! Essentially, Achan restated the arguments of the spies against Moshe's temporal authority, and those of Korach against Moshe's spiritual authority. Whereas the spies and Korach challenged Moshe in the second year of Moshe's tenure, Achan challenged Yehoshua in the second *month* of Yehoshua's leadership. These were two populist arguments: Who are you to change the rules? And who appointed you altogether?

This was a major crisis that threatened to undermine Jewish national life almost as soon as the Jews entered the land of Israel. The contentions of the spies succeeded in destroying an entire generation, and the reasoning of Korach almost succeeded – but for God's intervention – in turning the entire nation against Moshe. Achan appealed to the people as an ideologue, that they should recognize that power inheres in them, not Yehoshua, and that they would have fallen under the wheels of tyranny but for his self-sacrifice. Achan proposed that every Jew exercise the democratic right to pass judgment on the leadership, loudly and vociferously. There is nothing as

---

26. Essentially saying, "it's not the money, it's the principle."
27. Based on Bamidbar Raba 23:6, and *Me'avoor Ha'aretz*, page 83.

attractive to citizens in a free society as the uninhibited right to denounce their leadership – especially if there are no consequences to them.

How did Yehoshua respond? "My son," this is firstly a dispute among family members, do not exacerbate the problem. "Please give honor to Hashem, and confess to Him. Tell me please what you have done, do not withhold anything from me."[28] Secondly, do not impugn the integrity of the lottery system, because such a system will be used to divide the land of Israel among the tribes. At the very least, admit that the lot is accurate and reliable. There is no other way to equitably determine who gets what parcel in the land of Israel, and if people lose faith in the lottery we will never be able to dwell in the land. Neither you nor I can effectively decide how the land will be fairly distributed, and that is why the lottery system – based on the divine will – was in place.

It was a brilliant political maneuver. Yehoshua said that the lottery benefits everybody. If the people were inclined to accept the lottery for the distribution of the land, they would certainly accept it for the determination of the identity and fate of a single malefactor. In one swift stroke, Yehoshua validated the lottery as the most impartial means of allocating the land, and thereby deprived Achan of his following and his most compelling argument. Achan realized that if the people do accept the *goral* – and they *must* regarding the allocation of the land of Israel – they will accept its conclusions regarding his fate as well. Yehoshua legitimized the *goral* as the most equitable system, and in front of the people ratified the involvement of Providence in these affairs. When Korach rebelled, God Himself had to confirm Moshe's authority through the earthquake that swallowed Korach and his followers; here, Yehoshua accomplished the same goal by persuading Achan to validate the *goral* as the revealed will of Hashem.

After Achan authenticated the lottery, Yehoshua induced Achan to reveal all his crimes, and Achan was exposed not as an ideologue motivated by love of Torah but as a scoundrel who committed a number of crimes motivated by greed, arrogance and contempt for Torah. Like Korach, Achan's grievances were personal and petty – not philosophical. Achan had stolen the "Babylonian garment" – the cloak of the king of Bavel taken from the king's summer home in Yericho[29] – and thereby proclaimed to everyone

---

28. Tanchuma, Mas'ei 5, cited in *Me'avoor Ha'aretz*, page 80.
29. Rashi, Yehoshua 7:21, based on the Midrash, Breisheet Raba 5:15.

his pretensions to the throne of Israel. Suddenly, the force of Achan's arguments dissipated, and he succumbed.

Achan sought power, and his path to power was paved with the arrogance of the separatist. The rules that govern the lives of all men did not apply to him, especially the laws of the Torah. Thus Chazal perceived that Achan invariably committed a host of sins – violating all the Torah's laws (i.e., he excluded himself from the group that had accepted the Torah unanimously at Sinai), hiding his circumcision (i.e., he did not identify himself with his group of fellow travelers, *Klal Yisrael*), and ravaging a young bride (i.e., he asserted the right to seize anything for himself, even a maiden betrothed to another man).[30] Some Jews renounce their Jewish identity and fancy themselves citizens of the world; Achan renounced his Jewish identity and fancied himself a citizen of his own world.

Achan was a freethinker who advocated individual autonomy. He was not at all bound by the Torah system. The ultimate "autonomy" for the Jew is the repudiation of his membership in the Jewish people. He purported to sever his ties with the Jewish people by removing the distinctive mark of the male Jew, the *mila*. He bore no allegiance to any group beyond his own tribe.

He also chafed at the denial of the monarchy that should rightfully be his privilege or that of his tribe. This nourished a permanent sense of deprivation as well as entitlement; no pleasure could be denied him. In Chazal's lexicon,[31] the greatest act of selfishness and impudence is the violation of the *na'arah me'urasa*, the betrothed maiden who is merely awaiting the completion of the last stage of the marriage process before consummating the marriage with her intended husband. Achan's personality brooked neither self-control nor recognition of the rights of others. He grabbed whatever he wanted whenever he wanted because he was… Achan.

Conversely, Yehoshua, upon hearing of the defeat at Ai, first tore his clothing. If Jews were killed in Ai because of the sins of the generation, then he as the leader was personally responsible. He did not need a commission to investigate the catastrophe, nor was he looking for some contrived absolution from the media or his peers. "And Yehoshua tore his garments and fell on his face to the ground before the Ark of Hashem

---

30. Sanhedrin 44a.
31. See, e.g., R. Chiya's statement in Pesachim 49b.

until evening, he and the elders of Israel, and they placed dirt upon their heads" (Yehoshua 7:6). True leaders when confronted with failure do not seek refuge in disinformation, dissembling, distractions, or scapegoating. Yehoshua stood up, took the heat, and blamed himself for the failure at Ai. He grieved, mourned, and then began searching for the hidden spiritual flaw that had allowed this tragedy to occur.

The Gemara (Sanhedrin 44a) implies that thirty-six Jews were not killed at Ai, but only one – Yair ben Menashe – whose spiritual greatness was the equivalent of a Sanhedrin majority. The Meiri[32] commented that this means that the Sanhedrin was responsible for maintaining the religious integrity of the Jewish people, not only for the revealed sins that are under their explicit jurisdiction but also for their hidden sins. The influence of the Sanhedrin was such that they were obligated to uphold the spiritual level of the people. As best they could, the Sanhedrin had to know what was lurking in the heart of every Jew – what questions, flaws, heresies, vulnerabilities, or doubts. Yair ben Menashe symbolized the entire Sanhedrin and the institutional failure that took place. If an Achan could exist among the Jewish people, a miscreant whose despicable character was apparently unchanged through the years and miracles of the sojourn in the wilderness and the entry into the land of Israel, then it necessarily was a spiritual flaw in the people to which the Sanhedrin was insensitive. That flaw had to be uprooted.

Paradoxically, Yair ben Menashe's death reinforced Achan's heretical, self-centered beliefs. If even a righteous person like *Yair* can die in battle, then there are no guarantees in life, each person should seize whatever pleasures he can. It made no sense to attach oneself to a people and their concerns or battles, or to sacrifice one's life for any cause beyond self-preservation.[33] As the accommodationists of the 1940s and 1950s said: "Better Red than dead."

Achan's contempt for Yehoshua and for his brethren was nourished by the frustration of his royal ambitions. The Navi twice traced Achan's ancestry to Zerach, one of Yehuda's twin sons born to him and Tamar. "And it happened as she gave birth, one child put out a *hand*; the midwife took a crimson thread and tied it on his *hand* saying, 'this one emerged first.' And

---

32. Commentary of Meiri, Sanhedrin 44a.
33. *Me'avoor Ha'aretz*, page 83.

it was, as he drew back his *hand*, and behold his brother emerged. And she said, 'you have asserted yourself with strength,' and he was called Peretz. And then his brother came out, on whose *hand* was the crimson thread, and he called his name, Zerach" (Breisheet 38:28–30). Zerach, and the dynasty of Zerach, harbored a grudge against the Jewish people. A presumptuous Peretz, who breached the norms of childbirth and jumped ahead of his brother, robbed them of the kingship. But only one descendant acted upon this grievance: Achan.

Achan is twice described as "Achan, son of Carmi, son of Zabdi, son of Zerach, of the tribe of Yehuda" (Yehoshua 7:1 and 7:18). But when he was taken out for execution, Achan is identified in a simpler, more direct way: "And Yehoshua took Achan the son of Zerach" (7:24). He acted as the heir of his disgruntled ancestor, and lost everything.

The Midrash[34] noted that the Torah used the word *hand* four times in depicting the birth of Zerach. "Four times, corresponding to the four times that Achan stole or the four objects that Achan stole," the four times that Achan unlawfully stretched forth his hand to pilfer what was not rightfully his in an attempt to right the historical wrong done to his family.

This attack on Yehoshua's authority by a Jew who claimed that Yehoshua was the usurper and he, Achan, was the legitimate ruler was extremely dangerous, notwithstanding how common it is in our day. There are numerous people who feel they are worthy and entitled to leadership (whether political or spiritual),[35] and sometimes only seek leadership so that someone else should not lead. In most of the democratic world – particularly in the United States and Israel – there is an ongoing and relentless attack on political leaders and authority figures, to the point where it is almost impossible to conceive of a politician who is beyond reproach, and not a bum, a rogue, a crook, a charlatan, or worse.[36] But this attitude – albeit sometimes accurate – undermines every leader's ability to govern effec-

---

34. Yalkut Shimoni, Yehoshua, 18.
35. Chaim Weizmann, upon meeting Harry Truman after the State of Israel was established, told him that he, Weizmann, was a more important president than Truman. Questioned by Truman, Weizmann explained: "You are the president of 170,000,000 people, but I am the president of a million presidents." (*The Presidents of the United States and the Jews,* by David Dalin and Alfred J. Kolatch, Jonathan David Publishers, 2000, page 184–185)
36. The political commercials of all parties usually confirm this assertion!

tively, as *ab initio* his motivation to do anything is always suspect, and also discourages virtuous people from seeking positions of leadership.[37] Such an approach is anathema to Jewish life, and, notwithstanding its familiarity to us, had to be eradicated here at the very beginning of Jewish national life in the land of Israel.

"And Yehoshua took Achan the son of Zerach and the silver, the garment, the bar of gold and his sons and daughters and his ox, donkey, flock, tent and all that was his, and all Israel was with him. And they brought them up to the valley of Achor" (Yehoshua 7:24). The Gemara (Sanhedrin 44a) questioned why Achan's children were brought also. "If he sinned, how did they sin?" One opinion states that the children, and Achan's wife, knew of his crimes and shared his guilt. The Gemara concluded, though, that the children were brought along to intimidate them, so that they should witness their father's fate and understand his crimes and malevolence, and especially to uproot any sense of deprivation they might have. Achan's children had to see his punishment, so they would become subservient to the community and recognize that the fate of all Jews is intertwined.

Indeed, one opinion (not normative *halacha*) even claims that the children too were executed, as the ultimate deterrence. With that statement, Chazal impressed upon us how even one individual can be so destructive to a society, its internal harmony and the fulfillment of its destiny. We recognize more clearly how one person can corrupt and tear asunder a family; one demagogue – armed with ambition, followers, populist arguments and nefarious motives – can also destroy a community and the fabric of society.

Such a person has to be exposed and rooted out. Rashi[38] held that Achan was executed for Shabbat desecration, that despite the grave threat he posed to the body politic of Israel Achan was convicted of a "technicality," so to speak, a violation of one of the capital crimes of the Torah. The Rambam[39] disagreed and maintained that Achan was killed by Yehoshua – without witnesses or trial and based on his own confession, all deviations from normal legal procedure – extralegally, as either *hora'at sha'ah* (an

---

37. As in the well-known saw that "being a Rabbi is no job for a good Jewish boy."
38. Rashi, Yehoshua 7:25.
39. Rambam, Hilchot Sanhedrin, 18:6.

emergency measure) or through *din malchut* (the royal prerogative, because Achan was a *mored b'malchut*, a rebel against the king).

The individual has tremendous power to influence society – either to strengthen it or weaken it. And the same society can – and does – include great and lowly people in one generation. The Midrash[40] commented that the Divine Presence sings "'I am blackened' through Achan, but 'I am beautiful' through Yehoshua." One society can contain an Achan who is a greedy, egotistical, rebellious sinner, as well as a Yehoshua who is a righteous, selfless, faithful leader.

A different Midrash[41] emphasized this point in a remarkable way. "Why was the Decalogue conveyed to the Jewish people in the singular pronoun, not the plural?"[42] If we are so responsible for one another that we recite the *Viduy* confessional prayer in the plural ("we sinned"), perhaps the Torah should have been given not to every individual but to the assembly as a whole, in the plural? "Because any individual can nullify any of the Utterances, e.g., Achan nullified 'You shall not steal.'"[43] Even one person can tarnish the luster of a *mitzva*, and even one person can cool the waters and make sin more palatable, more acceptable and less horrifying. Each of the *Dibrot*, the foundational *mitzvot* of the Torah, deeply impressed the people – until each was violated at some point in Jewish history, and the aura of Sinai for that *mitzva* was then lost.

There was another long-term effect of Achan's sin. When a society has a pervasive and unbridled sense of personal autonomy, a disdain for authority, and an unlimited sense of entitlement, that society cannot long endure. The Midrash Talpiot[44] states that Achan sinned four times, stealing during the wars against Midian, Sichon, Og and Yericho. The first letters of the four "victims" of Achan spell out *masei* – journeys, a reference to "*Eileh masei Bnei Yisrael*," these are the journeys of the Children of Israel (Bamidbar 33:1). The first letters of the latter four words spell out the four exiles of the Jewish people after our entry to the land: Edom, Media, Bavel (Babylon) and Yavan (Greece).

---

40. Midrash Shir HaShirim Raba, 1:5.
41. Psikta Rabbati (Ish Shalom), Chapter 21.
42. "I am the Lord Your God… You shall not murder…" Each usage of "you" is singular in the Hebrew original.
43. The Psikta records how each of the *Dibrot* was nullified by a particular individual.
44. Quoting *Megaleh Amukot*, and cited by the *Mishbetzot Zahav*, page 151.

In other words, Achan's sin foreshadowed the future exile of the Jewish people from the land of Israel.[45] Because of Achan's sin, our conquest of the land was tainted, and therefore could never serve as a permanent conquest. The first sanctification of the land was thus only a temporary one and did not endure.[46] The sanctification itself was annulled by the Babylonian conquest. Achan's sin continued a tragic pattern of one person or small group (the worshippers of the golden calf, the spies, Korach, etc.) sinning shortly before the moment of triumph, deflating the hopes of the people, and abruptly halting the redemptive process.

The sin of Achan planted within the Jewish people the seeds of the disintegration of our national life in Israel. First, Achan spearheaded the threat of individual autonomy and the factionalization of our people. Achan posited that we are not a community with a common mandate and mission, but a group of individuals with distinct and often contrasting interests. Achan's private life was his own, and he thumbed his nose at society. He even had no interest in the theft itself. Not only was he by his own admission wealthy, but he also buried his bounty *under his tent* (Yehoshua 7:21). His tent was his castle, off-limits to anyone else. Achan derived pleasure from flouting authority. He was a civil war waiting to happen.

Second, he sneeringly rejected the authority of Torah, and made himself his own authority. His passions were his guide, and his intellect provided the rationalization. He had no concept of holiness, of limits, of the parameters of being a part of a "kingdom of priests and a holy people," nor any sense of being a member of Hashem's "treasured nation" (Shemot 19:5-6).

Third, he embodied the unrestrained materialistic impulses that sullied the purity of the conquest of the land. He attempted to transform us into conquerors like all conquerors, which deprived us of Hashem's protective hand and left us subject to the whims and fortunes of future conquerors. Avraham built an altar when he entered the land to pray that his descendants not stumble through the sin of Achan.[47] His activities in the land were paradigms for the virtuous events in our future, as well as warnings about the potential hazards we would face. A *mizbeiach*, an

---

45. The *trop*, cantillation, on the word "*Eileh*" is *azla gereish*, literally "he went and was driven out."
46. Masechet Shevuot 16a; Rambam, *Hilchot Bet HaBechira* 6:16.
47. Breisheet 12:8, with Rashi's commentary.

altar, is a structure that human beings build to consecrate the material land to God's service. It is often, literally, an elevation of the earth.[48] Our possession of the land is dependent on our capacity to elevate the earth, to consider the land of Israel as sacred – as the place divinely chosen for our residence – and as the place where the Torah's commandments are to be fulfilled and the ideal Torah society created.

Avraham elevated the earth to God's service, so his descendants should not construe the land of Israel as a Middle Eastern version of Peru or Portugal. This is a lesson not yet fully learned, and the essence of the internal struggle in Israel today. Is it to be a Jewish state or merely a state of Jews? And if it will be the latter, can it survive the internal turmoil and the external threats? The relative rates of *aliya* and *yerida* (immigration and emigration), and the sharpness of the religious and political divisions in the State of Israel today, indicate that the essential identity of the state is the key factor in determining one's responses to the great issues of the day: the role of Torah and *halacha* in the state, the attachment to the land itself and the willingness to renounce sovereignty over part of it, the readiness to defend it at all costs, and the very definition of citizenship in the Jewish state. The difference is fundamentally between those who trace Israel's history just to the nineteenth century, and those who connect the modern incarnation of Jewish nationhood with God's eternal covenant with our forefathers and the vision of the prophets. The latter perceive an intrinsic dimension to the land that shapes their entire worldview, whereas the former increasingly struggle to justify Israel's existence and the Jewish people's right to any part of the land.

After the execution of Achan, Yehoshua was now forced to restate the mission of Israel, and so he added the second paragraph of the *Aleinu* prayer, beginning "*Al ken nekaveh*," therefore we hope. The first three letters of those words spell out the name Achan, a daily reminder of Achan's sin,[49] its consequences, and our eternal calling "to perfect the universe through the Almighty's sovereignty, so that all mankind will call upon

---

48. Breisheet 8:20, with commentary of R. Shamshon Raphael Hirsch. Rav Hirsch's given Hebrew name – by which he was called to the Torah – was "Shamshon" – not Shimshon (as we heard from his great-grandson and namesake, the late Shamshon (Samson) Breuer.)
49. *Mishbetzot Zahav*, page 151, citing Midrash Talpiot.

Your name."[50] Yehoshua perceived that Achan's sin had caused a terrible breach in the holiness of the community and the commitment to our mission, and enunciated our "hope to soon see Your mighty splendor" and the implementation of Your mighty reign.[51]

One day, our possession of the land of Israel will presage an era of *tikun olam*, perfection of the world, through the perfect society we create there. That goal, which Achan tried to abort in its infancy, still remains for us to accomplish. Its complete realization awaits the coming of Moshiach, may He come speedily and in our days.

Summary

Our possession of the land is dependent on the realization that all Jews are interconnected, and guarantors one for the other. Each Jew must find his personal fulfillment within the context of national life, as part of his surrender to God's will. Achan betrayed those values, and represents the Jew who seeks to escape his destiny and renounce his heritage in order to satisfy his personal ambitions and cater to his subjective interpretation of the Torah. Achan is thus a ubiquitous threat to the stability of the Jewish nation.

---

50. *Aleinu* prayer.
51. Ibid.

⸺ Chapter Six
THE TREATY WITH GIVON

THE IMMEDIATE RESPONSE to the sin of Achan was the swift and comprehensive destruction of the city and people of Ai. Yehoshua sent a small decoy force to Ai, slightly northwest of Yericho, with the two main divisions ambushing Ai from the flank. The people of Ai fought, but with utter futility. The army of Israel suffered no casualties, and twelve thousand people – the entire population of Ai – were killed in battle. The city was set on fire, and the king of Ai was unceremoniously hanged towards evening. The spoils – animals and booty – were seized, as Hashem had commanded.[1] It was the first "conventional" military victory in the land of Israel.

Yehoshua immediately built an altar on Mount Eval, bordering the ancient city of Shechem, and inscribed on its stones a "repetition of the Torah" which the Ramban[2] interpreted as a listing of the 613 commandments. With two groups of six tribes standing respectively on Mount Eval and Mount Gerizim, and Yehoshua poised in the valley between, Yehoshua reenacted the ceremony described in the Torah – the public proclamation of the blessings and curses of the Torah that are the parameters of Jewish life.[3] The entire Torah was read to the entire congregation – men, women and children – and the destiny of the Jewish people was embraced with

---

1. Yehoshua, Chapter 8.
2. Ramban, Devarim 27:3.
3. Devarim, Chapter 27.

love and enthusiasm. The conquest of the remainder of the land of Israel was at hand.

As the people of Israel began the battle for the land of Israel, what military and diplomatic strategies did they follow? More precisely, was war the only option? What if a particular foe, witness to the supernatural events accompanying our entry to the land, sued for peace? What would have happened if a nation or tribe surrendered? Did the vanquished have the right to remain in the land of Israel, and under what circumstances? Generally, what are the rights of non-Jews who desire to live in the Jewish state? The framework for this discussion was the fateful treaty with Givon, which Yehoshua was duped into signing. There are aspects of that treaty that haunt us until today. What happened?

The Jewish Strategy of Conquest
The Torah outlined the diplomatic and military campaigns to be employed by the Jewish army of conquest. "When you draw near to a city to wage war against it, you shall call out to it for peace" (Devarim 20:10). The Jewish army is not allowed to go to battle without first making overtures for peace. Peace, though, means the enemy's unconditional surrender. "And it shall be that if it responds to you in peace and opens for you, then the entire people found there *shall be a tribute for you, and they shall serve you*" (Devarim 20:11). The capitulated enemy is pressed into service and becomes a tributary to the conqueror.

> But if it does not make peace with you, but makes war with you, you shall besiege it. Hashem shall deliver it into your hand, and you shall smite all its males by the sword. Only the women, children, animals and everything that shall be in the city – all its booty – may you plunder for yourselves; you shall consume the booty of your enemies, which Hashem gave you. So shall you do to all the cities that are very distant from you, which are not of the cities of these nations. But from the cities of these peoples that Hashem gives you as an inheritance, you shall not let any person live. (Devarim 20:13–16)

Those Canaanite tribes must be completely exterminated, "so that they will not teach you to act according to their abominations that they performed for their gods, so that you will then sin to Hashem, your God" (Devarim 20:18). For sure, the command to annihilate an entire people is jarring to our modern sensibilities. We are mindful of history's wars of extermination (which have often targeted Jews). The ethical dimension raised is – and should be – somewhat unsettling. Rav Shamshon Raphael Hirsch argued that such a command seemed ruthless even to the generation of the wilderness, and was incompatible with the ordinary moral strivings of the Jewish people. "The repeated admonitions not to have any mercy on the Canaanite population shows how much such a merciless procedure goes against the grain of the Jewish people and is against what they are meant to be, which is, and is to remain, the predilection to protect all living creatures. They are of regard this merciless procedure against the Canaanite population as an exception, expressly commanded by God, to be done at His bidding because of the special circumstances."[4] As such, an offer of peace always had to be extended, for the alternative to a peaceful surrender is total war.

Rashi[5] seemingly disagrees, commenting that an offer of peace is extended only in an optional war, but in an obligatory war – such as against Canaan or Amalek – the only initiative is the sword, until the enemy is vanquished and annihilated. And the Torah is adamant: if the Canaanite nations were not destroyed, they would ensnare the Jewish people in their deviant and decadent practices, and our residence in the land would be jeopardized. The land of Israel must be a holy place, a model society that is entirely free of any idolatry or primitivism. Any commitment to a non-Torah value system is anathema to the Jewish state and cannot be tolerated. And the mere presence of any idolatry renders our possession of the land very tenuous.

The Canaanite tribes stood out in their corruption, and special laws were enacted to deal with them. "You shall not seal a covenant with them, nor show them any favor" (Devarim 7:2). No treaties were allowed with Canaan, nor were any of the tribes to be allowed any permanent residence in the land.[6] No peaceful option was even to be explored during this first conquest of the land of Israel, according to Rashi.

---

4. Commentary of Rav Hirsch, Devarim 7:16.
5. Rashi, Devarim 20:10.
6. Rashi, Devarim 7:2, citing Masechet Avoda Zara 20a. This measure's applicability to non-Canaanite nations is part of today's dispute over the propriety or prohibition of surrendering Jewish land to the Arabs.

Rambam[7] disagrees, and argues that suing for peace is the standard offer made by the Jewish army against all adversaries, whether in an optional war or an obligatory war. Even the Canaanite nations were offered peace, with a third condition added to servitude and tribute: the tribe must accept the seven Noachide laws,[8] which acceptance effectively negates the Torah's concern that these tribes would constitute a moral hazard to the Jewish people.

In Rambam's formulation, if the proffered hand of peace is spurned then every member of the seven Canaanite nations is to be killed, whereas in a war with an optional enemy only the males are killed. But if any of these nations surrender, they may then reside in the land of Israel as adjuncts to the society – observing the Noachide laws and serving the Jewish people but possessing no national rights. If their religion is not idolatrous, they may even have a limited right of worship.[9] The obvious advantage to these non-Jews would be the privilege of living, even as subordinates, in a moral society that guaranteed their lives and strove to actualize the spiritual and intellectual potential in every human being.

The dispute between Rashi and the Rambam is fundamental on this point. Were the seven nations offered peace? What if one indigenous tribe or another sued for peace on their own? What should have been – and what was – Yehoshua's response? These questions and issues are at the heart of the Givon affair.

The kings of Canaan heard of the defeat of Ai and gathered together – unanimously – to protect their homeland against the Jewish onslaught (Yehoshua, Chapter 9). There was nothing unusual or particularly troubling about this response. It is what Yehoshua had expected, and such straightforward conflicts are relatively easy to fight. An enemy who is not reconciled to one's rights or claims, who masses his troops and is eager for war

---

7. Rambam, *Hilchot Melachim* 6:1.
8. Enumerated in Sanhedrin 56a: Prohibitions against murder, sexual immorality, idolatry, theft, blasphemy, eating a limb torn from a living animal, and an injunction to establish a judicial system. These are the basic norms of morality incumbent on every civilized society.
9. This is another pressing and relevant issue today, as most authorities maintain that Islam is not an idolatrous religion, and so Moslems would inherently possess the right to dwell in the land of Israel – but for their unyielding hatred, their relentless and merciless wars against the Jewish people and their rejection of our sovereign rights in the land of Israel.

is an adversary who can be confronted directly, forcefully and with great popular support. It is accepted that war is inevitable; the only unknown is the war's outcome, but here Yehoshua and his people were already privy to that information.

As we are witnessing in our day, it is much more complicated to combat an enemy who speaks the language of peace, friendship and morality. The Arabs of 1967, who in the wake of their debacle in the Six-Day War unabashedly proclaimed the "three no's of Khartoum" (no recognition of Israel, no negotiations with Israel, and no peace with Israel), were a simple enemy to demonize and ostracize. They embraced a platform of implacable hostility and rejection, and all Israelis knew where they stood and how that Arab hatred needed to be countered.

Already in the 1970s – and certainly by the 1990s – the Arabs began mouthing the right words, with the sincerity of those words in the ears of the beholder (or listener). Israeli society came apart in the 1990s over this very issue: were the Arabs duplicitous in their speech and gestures, and attempting to lull Israel into a fatal complacency and strategic vulnerability – or had they turned an honorable corner in unequivocally accepting the Jewish people's sovereign right to the land of Israel? Certainly, all Jews prefer peace, and many were willing to grasp at any rhetorical straw and exploit any sliver of opportunity to endorse the latter formulation. Even after years of relentless Arab terror should have divested any rational thinker of this notion, it still had its adherents. That this remains so at this late date – the peaceniks, at the lowest point, always console themselves that perhaps a "new leadership" or the "next generation" of Arabs will be more responsive[10] – is testament not only to the Jewish yearning for peace and the unconquerable nature of this fantasy, but also to the difficulty in contending with an enemy who uses the words of peace to mask his evil designs, or reveals his true intentions to Arabs in Arabic while saving his

---

10. Witness the outpouring of support and sympathy for the new Palestinian leader Mahmoud Abbas after the death of his mentor, Yasser Arafat, in 2004. Abbas served Arafat faithfully for more than *forty years*, and yet he is assumed to represent a radical departure from the brutality and depravity of his predecessor. This assumption underlies the wishful thinking of the segment of Israeli society that believes that peace is always an agreement or two away, and is thus prone to devastating lapses in judgment.

peaceful pronouncements for the Western world in English – a familiar tactic for the last twenty-five years.

A war that clearly delineates good and evil is easier to wage, but when good and evil are blurred by double vision and drowned out by double-talk, the struggle becomes more and more difficult to define or to support. King David already referred to this problem: "Hashem, rescue my soul from lying lips, from a deceitful tongue… Long has my soul dwelled with those who hate peace. I am peace – but when I speak, they are for war" (Tehillim 120:2, 6–7).

The kings of Canaan wanted to rumble, and for that Yehoshua was prepared. He was not prepared for the proposition of Givon, "who heard what Yehoshua had done to Yericho and to Ai" (Yehoshua 9:3). The Navi related that Givon[11] acted with guile and cleverness, and presented themselves to Yehoshua as ambassadors from a distant land who had just completed a long, arduous journey. "They disguised themselves, they took worn-out sacks for their donkeys, worn and cracked wineskins, worn and patched shoes, and worn garments on themselves… All their bread was dry and toasted" (9:4–5).

They approached Yehoshua with this offer: "We have come from a distant land, now seal a covenant with us" (9:6). The Jews were suspicious at first ("perhaps you dwell in our midst, how can I seal a covenant with you?" [9:7]) but shortly succumbed to the entreaties of these emissaries – impressed by their knowledge of recent Jewish history, duped by their disguise, and solicitous of their offer to become servants of Israel. "The men [of Israel] accepted their deceptive words, and did not inquire of Hashem. Yehoshua made peace with them, and sealed a covenant with them to let them live; the leaders of the congregation swore to them" (9:14–15).

It was not long – a mere three days – before the deception was revealed and Yehoshua learned that these messengers actually dwelled in the land of Israel, a short distance from the camp of Israel. Yehoshua confronted them in Givon, and realized he was trapped. He could not attack them, because the Jews had sworn to them that they would not be attacked. Nor could he sanction the treaty, because the Torah had explicitly banned such

---

11. Abravanel notes here that the Navi described them as "the inhabitants of Givon," rather than the king of Givon who apparently was inclined to join his fellow kings. The "inhabitants" acted unilaterally, in defiance of their king, sensing that they could not win this war. They acted out of a desire for self-preservation.

arrangements. Yehoshua castigated them for their deception, and a compromise of sorts was found: "Now you are cursed; slaves will never cease from among you – the woodchoppers and water drawers for the House of My God" (9:23).

Givon justified the trickery, saying that they heard that God had given Israel the land and had commanded Moshe to exterminate all the inhabitants. They were simply fearful of being massacred and subjugated themselves to Yehoshua's authority. And Yehoshua again designated them as woodchoppers and water drawers for the House of God and the altar (the Tabernacle) "until this very day"[12] (9:27). Indeed, as long as the Tabernacle stood, the men of Givon provided the wood and water.

Questions

Questions abound on this strange episode. The motives of the people of Givon seem pure. They knew they could not win this war and so were unwilling to die for a lost cause. What did they do wrong? Arguably, they nobly attempted to avoid a bloody conflict. Where is the harm in all this, such that it earns them Yehoshua's eternal curse?

Why was it necessary for Givon to deceive the men of Israel? This is not a question according to Rashi's opinion, which apparently does not allow for a negotiated solution to the wars against Canaan. But according to the Rambam, peace was always offered – in every conflict. Why did the Givonim not simply sue for peace – overtly and unambiguously?

Why were the Jewish people bound by an oath that was undertaken under false pretenses? The Jews thought that they were making a covenant with a foreign tribe, which was permitted under Torah law. When the hoax was exposed, why couldn't the Jews simply argue that the treaty, fraudulently negotiated, was null and void?

Israel's leaders demanded that the Givonim become woodchoppers and water drawers *"for the entire congregation"* (Yehoshua 9:21), whereas Yehoshua designated them for that same service but in *"the House of my God"* (9:23). What is the difference between the two resolutions?

Was this outcome a positive or a negative one for the Jewish people?

---

12. Malbim, Yehoshua 9:27, states that this refers to the day the Book of Yehoshua was written (mainly by Yehoshua himself, as per Bava Batra 15a).

Was the treaty with Givon good or bad, and what are its implications for today?

War and Peace

As noted above, Rambam[13] rules that peace must be offered to every enemy before hostilities are commenced, both before an optional or an obligatory war. If the enemy agreed to make peace and publicly accepted the seven Noachide laws, then they were allowed to live in Israel as non-citizens (essentially, legal resident aliens) with economic and civil rights. The main conditions were a renunciation of idolatry, the payment of tribute and a commitment to attend to the material needs of the Jewish society. They may then enjoy the spiritual bliss of living in the land of Israel, and are certainly free to leave the country at any time.

Accordingly, Rambam must hold that peace was offered to the Canaanite tribes; Rashi disagrees. How can we resolve this dispute?

The Gemara (Sotah 35b) discusses the Torah's requirement that the Jews plaster the words of the Torah and the *mitzvot* on two boulders at the entrance to the land. Rav Shimon added that underneath this extensive citation was the following verse: "So that they will not teach you to act according to their abominations that they performed for their gods, so that you will sin to Hashem, your God" (Devarim 20:18). The Gemara derives from this verse that "if the nations would repent, then we would accept them."

Rashi[14] explains that this verse was inscribed on the stones in order "to inform members of the seven nations who happened to dwell outside the land of Israel that we were only commanded to destroy Canaanites within the land so that we will not imitate their depravities, but you, who live outside the land, will be accepted if you repent. Resident Canaanites who repent cannot be accepted, for fear that their repentance is motivated not by sincerity but by fear." Thus, the war against Canaan was not ethnic but ideological; a foreign Canaanite was beyond the jurisdiction of the people of Israel and could even enter the land as long as he repudiated idolatry. Rashi maintains that peace was not an option with Givon.

---

13. Rambam, *Hilchot Melachim* 6:1.
14. Rashi, Sotah 35b.

Tosafot[15] ask a powerful question: If so, how did Yehoshua spare Rachav? She was a Caananite; so, notwithstanding her contributions to the war effort, on what halachic basis was she allowed to live? Tosafot answer that before the Jews crossed the Jordan, peace was offered even to these nations – and the injunction to slaughter the Canaanites only came into effect after we entered the land and the war began. Before we entered the land, the Canaanites were afforded the opportunity to repent and thereby save themselves. Rachav accepted the offer of repentance and peace, and was spared.

Tosafot continue that Yehoshua sent three messages to the enemy before conquest: "Those who wish to make peace can make peace; those who wish to make war can make war."[16] Clearly, even according to Rashi, peace must be – and was – offered before the war.[17] Rambam[18] goes further, stating that Yehoshua sent three diplomatic messages before entering the land, offering a choice of flight, peace, or war.

Why then did the Givonim engage in this subterfuge? If peace was offered, and ostensibly embraced,[19] why were they punished?[20]

Chazal offered several possibilities. According to Rashi, the Givonim had no choice but to deceive – as they failed to respond before the crossing of the Jordan, perhaps hedging their bets until they witnessed the fate of Yericho and Ai. According to most others, peace was possible but the Givonim miscalculated. Rambam stated that the Givonim at first did not accept the peace offer and, ignorant of Jewish law, were unaware that they could still make peace until the fighting actually started. Raavad[21] claimed

---

15. Tosafot, ibid.
16. Tosafot here do not record the third option, noted elsewhere: "Whoever wishes to leave can leave." Only one of the seven nations fled – the Girgashi – and they were rewarded with the continent of Africa.
17. Thus, according to all, peace must be offered before the conquest of the land started. According to Rashi, crossing the Jordan was the beginning of conquest, whereas according to Rambam, the commencement of open hostilities was considered the beginning of conquest.
18. Rambam, *Hilchot Melachim* 6:5.
19. Yerushalmi Shevuot 6:1 states that *"Givonim hishlimu,"* the Givonim made peace (in their own way).
20. Rambam (Hilchot Melachim 6:5) writes that the offer was made before the Jewish people crossed the Jordan River. Tosafot imply that the offer was extended before the war actually started.
21. Raavad's commentary on Rambam, ibid. This is similar to Rashi's approach.

that Rambam was mistaken, and that the Givonim resorted to trickery because the peace offer was only open until the Jews crossed the Jordan, which was tantamount to the beginning of the war. Once the Jordan was crossed, all bets were off. Tosafot[22] also held that the Givonim erred in their approach. It is true that peace was only offered before the war; nevertheless, although there is no obligation to accept a surrender offer after the war has already started, there is in such an instance no concomitant obligation to liquidate the enemy. In other words, the Givonim's late surrender offer might have been accepted by Yehoshua – but the Givonim did not know that.

Rav Hirsch proposed that the Givonim looked to negotiate a treaty on more favorable terms than the Torah offers, and so resorted to subterfuge.

Radak[23] suggested that the Givonim received Yehoshua's offer of peace, but thought it was a trap "offered as well to Yericho and Ai" in order to lull them into complacency. Cheaters and liars always assume that the world consists of other cheaters and liars, so the Givonim were unprepared to accept Yehoshua's word.

Clearly, then, the trickery of the Givonim was based on some misunderstanding. The question becomes: so what? Why was this matter so important that the Jews were distressed by it, such that some people wanted to kill the Givonim anyway, and Yehoshua cursed them so vehemently? And, if at the end of the affair, they became water drawers, wood carriers and worked in the *Mishkan*, what is the great harm?

The simple answer is that since our sojourn in the land of Israel was dependent on obeying the Torah, and the Torah explicitly prohibited making any covenant with the perverse residents of Canaan, then any covenant – even one made in error – weakened our hold on the land of Israel. It was not a political, diplomatic or military concern; rather, the introduction into Jewish society of an immoral and hostile element that rejects our value system must, over time, enervate the moral foundations of our community. The Jews did not merely fear the technical violation of one of the Torah's commandments, but the deleterious effects of this treaty on the future stability of our sovereign state.

---

22. Sotah, ibid.
23. Radak, Yehoshua 9:4. See, similarly, Malbim, Yehoshua 9:3.

Since the Givonim claimed to have arrived from a distant land and sought only a strategic agreement with Yehoshua, they were not asked to convert. They certainly gave no indication that they wished to reside in the land. When the deception was revealed, Yehoshua immediately realized the problem: there was now a fifth column that he had personally ushered into the land of Israel, a nation that merited destruction due to their despicable morals but which now had rights of residence in the land of Israel. What to do?

In his damage control Yehoshua again displayed his great wisdom. The princes of Israel wanted to scatter the Givonim throughout the society, as servants to the rest of the congregation. Yehoshua decided otherwise: "Let them be wood choppers and water drawers for the House of my God" (Yehoshua 9:23). The only way to minimize their potential spiritual harm was to have them work in the *Mishkan* or *Bet HaMikdash*, in the company of the *kohanim* and *Levi'im*. There they would be positively influenced by the holy environment, and gradually forsake their licentious tendencies.[24] It was a brilliant maneuver, even if it was not a complete success.

Yehoshua cursed them nonetheless, because he knew that this solution – although the best possible under the circumstances – was not ideal. Even though they would work in a sacred setting, the Givonim were still religious outsiders, not part of the ideological system of the Jewish people. The possibility of future trouble could never be ruled out – and, of course, the deception they perpetrated on the Jewish people was a constant irritant.

Why was Israel bound to an agreement that was fraudulently obtained? Rambam[25] ruled that "it is forbidden to equivocate in the covenant or lie [to the nations] once they have made peace and accepted the Noachide laws." Even if peace is achieved under false pretenses – assuming, of course, the adversary adheres to its side of the agreement – the agreement cannot be renounced, nor can the enemy be cheated in return. There *is* a double standard that demands higher ethical conduct from the Jewish people.

The Gemara (Gittin 46a) makes this point abundantly clear. "Rav Yehuda stated that any vow of which the public (either three or ten people) is aware cannot be retracted; hence, Yehoshua could not repudiate the cov-

---

24. For a short time, the *Mishkan* was even located in Givon.
25. Rambam, *Hilchot Melachim* 6:3.

enant with the Givonim." The Rabbis, who disagree with Rav Yehuda and permit the retraction of even a public vow under certain circumstances, maintain that the agreement with the Givonim never formally took effect. "So why didn't Yehoshua kill them? Because of the desecration of God's name [that would entail]." Tosafot comment that if not for the potential *chilul Hashem* – the nations would say the Jews cannot be trusted to keep their word – Yehoshua could have banished them from the land. Yehoshua's hands were literally tied by the principal mandate of Jewish life: to sanctify God's name through all our endeavors.

This point motivates, but also haunts us until today. When the Oslo Accords broke down in the mid-1990s in a wave of Arab terror, some Jewish voices urged a unilateral observance of the treaty's terms on the grounds of *chilul Hashem*. Even if the Arabs breached each and every one of their commitments (raising an army far larger than permitted, with more powerful weaponry, perpetration and support of terror, relentlessly hostile propaganda and inculcation of hatred against Jews and Israel, etc.), many held that it would be unbecoming and immoral for Israel to abrogate the Oslo treaty and neglect to carry out its obligations – primarily surrender of land and financial support to the Arabs – and cited the treaty with Givon as proof.

The analogy was flawed, primarily because the Givonim – although dishonest in obtaining the agreement – always adhered to its terms and willingly became servants of the Jewish people. Thus, Israel's paramount obligation to sanctify God's name precluded a renunciation of this treaty. But the Oslo Accords, while similarly procured through duplicity, were immediately breached by one of its two signatories. Why Israel for the next decade – through five prime ministers of different policies and temperaments – insisted on fulfilling its terms unilaterally is a mystery that future generations will undoubtedly explore but perhaps not unravel. Surely, it defied logic, common sense, the norms of diplomacy and elementary morality.

The duty of *kiddush Hashem* is fundamental to Jewish life – and the Givonim knew this, and knew how to exploit it. They cunningly took advantage of the Jews' yearning to magnify God's name in the world, and knew exactly the right words – the correct terminology – that would appeal to the Jewish people.[26] "Your servants have come from a distant land

---

26. *Mishbetzot Zahav*, page 179.

for the sake of Hashem, your God. We have heard of His fame and all He did in Egypt" (9:9). They essentially said that they have seen the light, they view world events precisely as we do, and therefore there is no reason for hostilities. They want what we want, to recognize the "obligation of all creatures to thank, praise, and extol" the Creator.[27] They pretended to adopt Yehoshua's own formulation in *Aleinu*, to be our partners "in perfecting the world under God's kingship."

It sounded good, even inspired, and the Jews capitulated – much as Jews today succumb to the doublespeak of our enemies, and the use of terms such as freedom, human rights, occupation, self-determination, and others.[28] The Givonim realized that they could not succeed on the battlefield, and so they attempted to defeat the Jews through diplomacy – finding the right verbiage that would cause us to forego our obligations, dilute our destiny, and betray our mission. They wished to induce a violation of the Torah, a deviation from our plan of attack, so that Jewish society would ultimately collapse from within. They were sneaky, like the primeval serpent that seduced Chava, the wife of Adam.

"If they were part of the Emori tribe, why were the Givonim referred to as *Chivi*? Because they behaved like a *chivi*,[29] like the serpent which seduced Chava with words… [They said:] 'We know the Torah prohibits Israel from enacting a covenant with the Canaanite tribes. So we will deceive them in signing a treaty. If they then kill us, they would have desecrated God's name. If they do not kill us, they would have violated the Torah's decree. In any event, they will be punished and we, the Givonim, will inherit the land.'"[30] Through their deviousness, the Givonim cornered Yehoshua – either Israel had to violate the Torah or desecrate the name of Heaven. Clever, indeed.

Yehoshua cursed them, just as the serpent was cursed. Just as the serpent desired Chava and schemed to seduce her, so too the Givonim desired the land of Israel and sought to obtain it deviously. Similarly, Shechem, the prince of the land, kidnapped and raped Yaakov's daughter

---

27. From *Shacharit*, on Shabbat.
28. For example, the demand that Israel, a sovereign country, provide consistent employment within its borders to a group of hostile noncitizens – Palestinians – defies logic, is unprecedented, and yet is internationally accepted as one of Israel's *obligations*.
29. *Chivi* derives from the word *chivya*, which means "snake" in Aramaic.
30. Midrash Bamidbar Raba 8:4. Also found in Yerushalmi Kiddushin 4:1.

Dina,[31] and then wanted to marry her in order to destroy Yaakov's family from within – through intermarriage. Givon too wanted to commingle with us and integrate into our society in order to draw us to idolatry, tear apart the fabric of Jewish society, and undermine our position in the land of Israel. Their goal was not peace; their goal was the destruction of the Jewish people. "Peace" was their tactic, and words were their weapons.[32] Like Bilaam, the Givonim knew that our rights to the land of Israel are inextricably linked to our observance of the Torah. Their tactic was indirect but ingenious: weaken the Jewish people's attachment to the Torah, and the land will gradually slip away from them.

Nothing in Jewish life compares to our eagerness to sanctify God's name and aversion to desecrating it. We will literally sacrifice our lives to accomplish either goal. As paradoxical as it sounds, Yehoshua's options were limited in dealing with this duplicitous foe. He had to worry – just like we have to worry – about a potential *chilul Hashem* because such would frustrate the very purpose of our existence; our enemies are unconcerned about this, except to know how to take advantage of this chink in our armor.

Chazal too, with their exquisite sensitivity to human affairs, perceived in the episode with Givon poetic justice for an unrectified blemish on Jewish life. After Shechem's marriage offer to Dina, Yaakov's sons proposed that the residents of Shechem first circumcise themselves to be worthy of Yaakov's family. They did, "and on the third day, when they were in pain, two of Yaakov's sons, Shimon and Levi, each took his sword, and they came upon the city confidently, and slew every male" (Breisheet 34:25). Yaakov was outraged, if only for the *chilul Hashem* caused by their deception, saying "you have made me odious in the eyes of the inhabitants of the land" (Breisheet 34:30). He said in effect that Shimon and Levi distorted the Torah and subjected it to ridicule, so that now people will think the Torah's commandments (like *mila*) are not laws designed to sanctify and ennoble our lives but are rather tools of deceit and deception used in order to exploit the nations. Yaakov could not abide this mutilation of the Torah's words and purpose.

This taint remained on Yaakov's descendants, until they were similarly

---

31. Breisheet, Chapter 34.
32. *Mishbetzot Zahav*, page 178.

victimized by a group, the Givonim, who also exploited the Torah's ideas in order to derive a material advantage. Yehoshua and the Jewish people were forced to accept these venomous outsiders in their midst, and live with the consequences.

Yehoshua apparently allowed them to convert but not fully integrate into Jewish life. They were denied the right to marry Jews. Radak[33] cites the Midrashic statement that the Givonim became wood hewers and water carriers "to the house of my God": "as long as the Temple exists, they cannot marry into the Jewish people." Yehoshua's temporary decree was ratified and made permanent by King David, who permanently barred them from marrying into the Jewish family. They were, indeed, second-class citizens, with an inferior lineage enunciated by Ezra and enshrined in *halacha*.[34] Why? For an answer, we must fast-forward four centuries into the future.

The Midrash[35] relates that the Jewish people were afflicted with a famine during David's time "because Shaul put to death the Givonim." But did he? Not in the literal sense. When David fled from King Shaul's murderous rage, he briefly sought refuge in Nov, the city of *kohanim* and site of the *Mishkan*. The *kohanim*, not knowing that David was a fugitive, supplied him with provisions, and when Shaul was so informed, he ordered that the inhabitants of Nov be killed. One tragic consequence of this mass murder, besides the obvious, was that it left the Givonim – who resided and worked in Nov, and were supported by the *kohanim* – bereft of any means of support. Impairing the earning capacity of the Givonim was construed in Heaven as a breach of the treaty, and akin to murdering them – justifying a famine in Israel. Radak maintained that Shaul took advantage of this opportunity to drive them from the country altogether, another violation of the treaty.[36] When David complained, Hashem responded: "If you further distance those who are already far, you will yet distance those who are close."

Why then did David drive them away? To make amends with the Givonim, David acceded to their request that they be allowed to hang seven

---

33. Radak, Yehoshua 9:21.
34. In Kiddushin 69a, the Givonim are referred to as *netinim* (literally, "given over" to service in the Temple) and ranked, so to speak, below *mamzerim*. See below.
35. Midrash Bamidbar Raba 8:4.
36. Radak, II Shmuel 21:1.

surviving members of Shaul's family.³⁷ They did, and left them hanging. That act of barbarism led David to conclude that the Givonim lacked the three basic traits of the Jew (compassion, humility and kindness), and he pronounced them unfit to enter the covenant of Israel.³⁸ By their actions, they proved themselves unworthy of the name Israel. More than four centuries of living in the proximity of the Sanctuary failed to change their basic natures. They were categorized as *netinim*, and neither their males nor females may ever marry a Jew.³⁹

This is unique, because Rambam⁴⁰ held that sincere converts were accepted even from the seven Canaanite nations. But only the Givonim sought to convert – insincerely – and David permanently banned their marriage to Jews "because he saw in them a brazenness and cruelty" in murdering the offspring of Shaul.⁴¹ Indeed, when the Jewish people appealed to the Givonim for assistance on the eve of the destruction of the first *Bet HaMikdash*, the Givonim turned a blind eye and a deaf ear.⁴²

For centuries, the Givonim existed in this ambivalent state. Even in the future, their basic personality – devious, cunning, aggressive, and uninspired by our culture or value system – will remain and they will never be able to join the Jewish people.⁴³ There can be residents of the land of Israel who will never reconcile themselves to our existence, and always remain beyond the pale of civilized society. They remain, in order to challenge and weaken our control of the land.

From the very beginning of the conquest of the land, the indigenous population always posed a danger to our survival. The Torah itself demands that conquest of the land requires the displacement of the degenerate and depraved local population; otherwise, "they will be for you pins in your eyes and thorns in your sides, and they will harass you... and what I meant to do to them, I shall do to you" (Bamidbar 33:55–56). As the commentator Rav Ovadia Sforno there notes: "If you do not eliminate them, then even

---

37. This strange story is recorded in II Shmuel 21:1–14. Apparently, the seven participated in the banishment of Givon or were otherwise guilty in Heaven's judgment.
38. Midrash Bamidbar Raba 8:4.
39. Yevamot 78b.
40. Rambam, *Hilchot Issurei Bi'ah* 12:22.
41. Rambam, ibid. 12:24.
42. *Mishbetzot Zahav*, page 191, citing the *Tisha b'Av kina* of Rav Elazar HaKalir, "shavat suru meni."
43. Tosafot, Bava Batra 122a.

though you will conquer the land you will not be able to bequeath it to your children… for you will surely stray after their false gods."

Yehoshua defeated thirty-one kings.[44] One nation, the Girgashi, fled. One nation, the Givonim, stayed under false pretenses and tormented the Jews for centuries. To host an antagonistic tribe with nationalistic pretensions, and which resents and rejects Jewish claims of sovereignty to the land of Israel, precludes not only peace but also stability, tranquility, and even a modicum of security. That is not to say that the mere removal of foreign, hostile elements brings peace and security; it is to say that the mere presence of foreign, hostile elements always engenders instability and insecurity. That is the dilemma that Yehoshua first confronted here, and that has bedeviled generations since – including our own.

It should be obvious that the land of Israel cannot sustain two nations with incompatible and mutually exclusive claims of sovereignty, but this point has, as yet, not penetrated the Jewish psyche or been accepted by most of the Jewish people. Hence, the endless pursuit of peace plans, schemes, conferences, initiatives, road maps, memoranda, understandings, accords – each with a place name or proper noun preceding it. And, above all, the immersion in a "peace process" that leads to ceremonies and treaty signings, and not much else that is productive or enduring.

Treaties, as we learned in dealing with Givon, will tie the hands of the Jewish people, but not necessarily our foes. We will be constrained – through our desire to avoid a *chilul Hashem* or even just as a consequence of our innate yearning for peace – to treat the signed document as sacrosanct, notwithstanding our realization that our enemies are sophisticated enough to use platitudes and flowery locutions as weapons of war, to sap our morale and rally the international community against the very notion of a Jewish state. Our enemies are not constrained at all by what they sign or the promises they make.[45]

The avoidance of *chilul Hashem* does not justify national suicide, and certainly requires an elementary fairness on the part of the observer. A potential *chilul Hashem* does not ordinarily require a Jew to unilaterally

---

44. Yehoshua, Chapter 12.
45. The 1996 Hebron Accords prohibited the Arabs from, among other things, possessing machine guns. Nonetheless, they celebrated the signing of the agreement by… wildly firing their machine guns in the air, blithely unconcerned that this was a flagrant violation of the agreement just signed.

surrender his rights and relinquish his just claims. It certainly does not require a renunciation of our rights to the land of Israel; on the contrary, that surrender and retreat might be *per se* a *chilul Hashem* (in accordance with Yechezkel 36:20).[46] And yet, the Jewish people are gripped – understandably so – by the desire to sanctify God's name and the revulsion at any possible desecration.

How can Tosafot[47] say that "the Givonim will never be cured, not even in the future" – especially if we posit that "Sancheriv came and mingled all the nations"?[48] The answer is that even at the end of days there will be a nation like the Givonim, who will attempt to draw near to us with their words and their professions of morality. They will decry the evils of nationalism generally (but only intend ours), they will mask their aggression with the rhetoric of religion, and they will urge all the so-called "monotheistic" religions to unite, but under their banner and at their behest.[49]

The Givonim represent that enemy of Israel who knows how to exploit our basic goodness, to shackle our hands with treaties that violate the Torah, weaken our resolve, and debilitate our defenses. Yehoshua's only solution was to attempt to bring them close to Torah. His plan did not succeed, and the Givonim and their spiritual descendants remain to vex us until today. Yehoshua failed to consult the *Urim v'Tumim* to ascertain the best approach – much as Shimon and Levi did not consult Yaakov in advance either. Some mistakes linger – sometimes for centuries, and sometimes for millennia.

The land of Israel is essentially a holy land; its sanctity is its defining characteristic. Its preservation is not dependent on uprooting this or that people but on uprooting and dislodging false ideologies. That, on occasion, requires destroying those nations that subscribe to those ideologies, which was the premise of the wars against Canaan. Thus, any individual or group that wished to renounce its corrupt doctrines was welcomed into the Jewish

---

46. "And they desecrated My holy Name when it was said of them, 'these are the people of Hashem, but they departed His land.'"
47. Tosafot, Bava Batra 122a.
48. Mishna Masechet Yadayim 4:4, Masechet Brachot 28a. Sancheriv, for strategic reasons, carried out a massive transfer of populations a generation before the destruction of the First Temple, leaving no Biblical nation with its original identity.
49. Egypt's Anwar Sadat often spoke of his desire to build a worship center for the three major "religions" at Jab-el-Musa in the Sinai desert – but only after Israel surrendered it to his control. He never did.

society. It is enough for the nations to abandon their idols – and they are our partners in *tikun olam* (perfection of the world); they need not convert to Judaism. They become part of the class of servants of Hashem who carry out His will and benefit all mankind.

Eventually, we will arrive at that moment. Until then, we find ourselves in Yehoshua's position – dealing with foreigners inimical to our religious and national destiny – and attempting to devise solutions that show no greater possibility of success than did his. The challenge then becomes moving forward and building a model Torah state, notwithstanding the difficulties, the perplexities and the uncertainties. Yehoshua's challenge when he entered the land of Israel is still our challenge as we return to the land of Israel.

Summary

The confrontation with Givon introduced the vexing issue of dealing with the indigenous non-Jewish population of the land of Israel, especially a population that understood how to exploit for its own nefarious ends the Torah, our goodness, and our yearning to sanctify God's name in the world. Yehoshua's resolution was the best under the circumstances, but the Givonim never fully assimilated into Jewish life and remained a troubling phenomenon that hindered the stability of the Jewish state.

Chapter Seven
MIRACLE AT GIVON

THE MIRACLE AT GIVON – when the sun stood still during the battle with the kings of the Emori tribe – is one of the most celebrated in the Bible. Yehoshua stood before the people, and declared: "Sun, stand still in Givon, and moon, in the Valley of Ayalon" (Yehoshua 10:12).[1] The question is: why was it necessary? It certainly was not a military necessity, as the miracle occurred after the Emori had already been routed and were fleeing the battlefield. At that point, Yehoshua requested the miracle, which essentially prolonged the day of combat. But for what purpose?

And how was this miracle different from other miracles? Ralbag commented that if we understand this miracle literally – the sun standing still for an extra day or so – then it would have had a global impact, its effect felt, for example, in a corresponding period of extended darkness in South America. That would quantify it as one of the greatest miracles ever, equal to if not greater than the splitting of the Red Sea, and surpassing even the miracles of Moshe which only affected limited areas. And certainly there was no greater miracle worker than Moshe "whom God had known face to face, as evidenced by all the signs and wonders that God sent him to perform in the land of Egypt…" (Devarim 34:10–11). Yehoshua the disciple could not exceed the supernatural accomplishments of Moshe.

Consequently, Ralbag maintains that the sun did not actually stand still but rather that the earth's rotation slowed down somewhat, so in fact

---

1. "Shemesh b'Givon dom, v'yareach b'emek Ayalon."

the sun shone a little longer that day. Most of the traditional commentators reject Ralbag's approach, and Abravanel[2] notes that the slowing of the earth's rotation is also a great miracle, in fact, the same miracle the Navi refers to explicitly. Rav Chisdai Crescas, a philosopher who preceded Abravanel by one generation, construed the miracle in completely naturalistic terms, as if the battle itself was hastened so the day appeared longer. That approach, too, is spurned by the traditional commentators. What did happen? What were the causes of this battle, and what was the significance of this miracle that finally secured our conquest of the land of Israel?

The Navi[3] relates that Adoni-Tzedek,[4] the king of Yerushalayim,[5] witnessed the fate of Yericho and Ai and the surrender of Givon and immediately tried to rally the support of his fellow kings. He sent word to the four kings dwelling south of Yerushalayim: "Come up to me and help me, and let us smite Givon, for it has made peace with Yehoshua and with the Children of Israel" (Yehoshua 10:4).[6]

The kings had no interest in fighting Yehoshua; they wanted to attack Givon because it had the audacity to break ranks with them and negotiate their own treaty with Israel. They had envisioned a Canaanite solidarity – a united rejectionist front against Israel – that Givon had breached, and now they wanted to topple Givon as a lesson to others. This certainly evokes, in our day, the widespread revulsion towards Egypt in the Arab

---

2. Abravanel, Yehoshua, Chapter 10.
3. Yehoshua, Chapter 10.
4. Chazal (Yalkut Shimoni Yehoshua, 19) note that all the kings of Yerushalayim until this point were always called Malki-Tzedek or Adoni-Tzedek, king or lord of justice, as Yerushalayim was known as the place of justice. Adoni-Tzedek here felt that a terrible injustice was being perpetrated against the Canaanite tribes.
5. Yehoshua 10:1. This is the first reference in *Tanach* to the city of Yerushalayim. In Breisheet 14:18, Malki-Tzedek the king of Shalem greets Avraham upon his triumphant return from the war against the kings. Yerushalayim is a compound word, consisting of *Yeru*, "they will see," the name Avraham gave to this place (Breisheet 22:14) and *Shalem*, "perfection," its initial name. The *yud* of Yerushalayim is usually dropped in *Tanach*, in order to maintain the integrity of the word *Shalem* (Tosafot, Taanit 16a, "Har"). Chida mentions that *Yeru* has the identical *gematria* – numerical value – as *Yireh*, "he will see."
6. Yehoshua was encamped at Gilgal, northeast of Yerushalayim, and Givon was located northwest of Yerushalayim, almost in the center of the country. These kings, who were situated to the south of Yerushalayim, feared that Yehoshua was coming for them next.

world after Egypt signed its treaty with Israel in 1979. Almost every Arab state severed diplomatic relations with Egypt for its ignominious act and its "crime" against the Arab people.[7] Here, the kings of Canaan presaged that event, and were outraged by the treachery of Givon.

Abravanel[8] states that the kings descried another ominous development. Peace had been made between Israel *"and the inhabitants of Givon"* (10:1), but not with the king of Givon. The people had risen up on their own initiative, in a profoundly precocious act of democratic self-expression, and concluded that they did not want to fight Israel or die in their king's futile wars. They negotiated a treaty on their own and essentially rejected the authority of their king. To the other despots of Canaan, this rebellion – with its democratic impulses – was a dangerous phenomenon that could not stand. If unchallenged, their own monarchies would be threatened - not by Yehoshua but by their own people. The kings united and marched against Givon.

Notwithstanding the devious circumstances of its treaty with Israel, Givon appealed to Yehoshua for military assistance: "Do not loosen your hands from your servants, come up to us quickly, save us and help us, for all the Emori kings who dwell in the mountains have gathered against us" (10:6). Malbim[9] explains that there is a difference between "save us" and "help us"; saving (*yeshua*) denotes a complete salvation, whereas help (*ezrah*) is a partial rescue. The Givonim requested both, like good diplomats – they desired the former but would settle for the latter.

Yehoshua responded immediately, moved his army to Givon, and then was seized by fear. Hashem pacified him: "Do not fear them, for I have

---

7. When it became apparent over the years that Egypt's peace treaty was in word only and did not mark any substantive change in its hostility towards Israel, most Arab states (aside from several rejectionists) restored diplomatic ties with Egypt. Since the mid-1990s, Egypt has had a sitting ambassador in Israel only sporadically, as the "cold peace" has grown even colder.
8. Abravanel, Yehoshua 10:1.
9. Malbim, Yehoshua 10:6. The *Mishbetzot Zahav* (page 190) notes interestingly that two leaders brought Jews into the land of Israel from the exile, Yehoshua and Ezra. Yehoshua's entry reflected his name ("God will save"), a complete salvation effected by Hashem through open miracles. When Ezra ("help") returned with a small group of Jews at the beginning of the Second Temple era, the people were unworthy of open miracles and so had to reconquer and resettle the land on their own. The divine assistance was natural, not miraculous, and the salvation was incomplete. The third return to Israel – in our day – is still awaiting a clear definition.

delivered them into your hand; not even one of them will stand against you" (10:8). But what did Yehoshua fear?

The Midrash[10] records that Yehoshua was tormented by one thought: "Should I impose on our community the burden of defending these insincere converts of Givon"? Was it worth committing our forces and risking Jewish life to defend these people who, with malice aforethought, had just deceived us? Hashem answered: Yes. "If you distance those who are already distant, you will ultimately distance also those who are near." Hashem's love for every Jew, and especially converts, must prevail. In truth, there is no person who is without blemish or flaw. Therefore, if one starts to discriminate between Jews based on some perceived shortcoming, eventually everyone will be subjected to bigotry. There will always be a reason why this Jew or that group of Jews does not measure up to "my" or "our" standards of perfection, and therefore does not deserve the protection of the community; perhaps it is their background, their level of scholarship or observance, or place of residence (in Israel, outside Israel, or some less-favored location even within Israel), or something else. And the Torah's fundamental mandate "You shall love your neighbor as yourself" (Vayikra 19:18) is a *commandment*, not just an ideal, essentially reflecting the reality that not every Jew is inherently lovable. Nonetheless, we are commanded by Hashem to love our fellow Jew – as an expression of our love for Him. We love all Jews, not just those who are lovable but especially those who are not (yet) lovable.

If such distinctions between people are made nevertheless, then it is a slippery slope indeed. Eventually the number of Jews worthy of universal protection will be whittled down to a very small class. But Hashem's goodness is unlimited, and "He does good for the wicked and the good."[11] Yehoshua was taught to emulate God in this respect. Not only were his fears misplaced, but as the leader of Israel he also was obligated to intervene on behalf of this less-favored group of (quasi-)Jews.

The unusual relationship with Givon was the first reason why the miracle here was necessary. In Hebrew, a *nes* (literally, miracle) also means

---

10. Midrash Bamidbar Raba 8:4.
11. V'chol maaminim, Yamim Noraim tefila, as cited by *Mishbetzot Zahav*, page 191. He quotes the famous statement of Reb Zushe of Anipol about himself, that "He wishes he had as much love for the greatest *tzadik* as Hashem has for the simplest Jew."

a banner or flag.[12] A *nes* is something that calls attention to God's presence on earth. The miracle at Givon focused people's minds on the war and the *kiddush Hashem* (sanctification of God's name) it engendered. It was a lesson to the nations that not only did the Jewish people refuse to nullify a treaty enacted under false pretenses, but we would even go to war to defend our new allies. The war took place amid supernatural effects so that it would surely be noticed and remembered. Yehoshua proclaimed "Sun, stand still in Givon," but the sun stood still not only in Givon but throughout the Middle East! The phrase, associated with Givon, would forever trigger memories of the battle, and who fought (Israel), and on behalf of whom they fought (Givon).

The Battle

> Yehoshua came upon them suddenly; he had descended from Gilgal all night. Hashem confounded them before Israel and smote them with a mighty blow at Givon. They pursued them by way of ascent to Bet Choron, and struck them until Azekah and until Makkedah. (Yehoshua 10:9-10)

The course of battle took Yehoshua westward from Gilgal to Givon, and then southwest, past Yerushalayim, to Bet Choron and environs.

> And it happened that when they fled before Israel, they were on the descent of Bet Choron when Hashem cast upon them large stones from Heaven until Azekah and they died. And more died through the stones of the hail than the Children of Israel killed with the sword. (Yehoshua 10:11)

The Navi describes the major weapon of war as *avnei habarad*, the stone of *the* hail, and not simply *avnei barad*, hailstones. The Midrash[13] relates that when Pharaoh of Egypt pleaded with Moshe to stop the plague of hailstones, Moshe acquiesced. "Moshe went out from Pharaoh from the city, and he stretched out his hands to Hashem; the thunder and hail ceased and rain did not reach the earth" (Shemot 9:33). The hail miraculously stopped in mid-air – only to continue its descent to earth (*the* identical hail) on the

---

12. "V'sa nes l'kabetz galuyotenu," raise the banner to gather our exiles (from the daily Amida).
13. Midrash Tanchuma, Va'era 16.

heads of the Emori fleeing Yehoshua's army. The Midrash adds that some of that hail still remains, and will reappear to destroy the armies of Gog of Magog in the apocalyptic war that will usher in the Messianic age.

Of course, Chazal were conveying not meteorological tips but a profound concept. There is a progression in Jewish life, an inherent link between seemingly disparate events. The Exodus from Egypt, which defined us as a people, was the initial stage in our national existence, and was confirmed through the hail from above. When the Jews entered the land of Israel, conquered the Emori (this was the climactic battle) and solidified our possession of the land – the second stage of our development – the hailstones again ratified our conquest. The third stage will be the rebirth of our nation at the end of days and our permanent conquest of Israel, and it will again be accompanied by the remnant of that same hail. All Jewish history is a continuum from Egypt to Sinai to Israel, to exile and back to Israel.

> Then Yehoshua spoke to Hashem on the day Hashem delivered the Emori before the Children of Israel, and he said before the eyes of Israel, 'Sun, stand still in Givon, and moon, in the Valley of Ayalon.' Then the sun stood still, and the moon stopped, until the nation took retribution against their enemies. Is it not written in the Book of the Upright, so the sun stood in the middle of the sky and did not hasten to set for a whole day. There was no day like that before it or after it, that Hashem heeded the voice of a man, for Hashem did battle for Israel. (Yehoshua 10:12–14)

The Miracle

What are miracles? The Midrash[14] quotes Rav Yonatan: "During the six days of creation, Hashem stipulated with His creations; with the sea that it should split when the Jewish people had to cross, and with the sun and the moon that it should stand still before Yehoshua, and with the lions that they should not harm Daniel, etc." According to the predominant opinion among the *Rishonim* (the medieval authorities), miracles are not spontaneous interventions of Hashem but were rather programmed into creation from the very beginning. During creation, Hashem ordained that

---

14. Midrash Yalkut Shimoni, Yehoshua, 21.

at a particular time (certainly according to His will), a technical deviation from the natural order would occur in order to benefit the Jewish people.

This, for sure, challenges the popular notion that miracles are unpremeditated divine acts – an opinion also reflected in the Midrash.[15] "The righteous are given dominion over what was created to illuminate the day and the night, as in the case of Yehoshua. He said to the luminaries, 'just as I am not silent in my study of Torah, so too you must now be silent in front of me.' Yehoshua continued that 'my ancestor (Yosef) dreamt that the sun and the moon bowed down. Now is the time to fulfill that vision.'" In essence, the master of the Torah is able to dictate to the natural world. Yehoshua appealed to Hashem for this miracle, and Hashem responded favorably.

This fundamental dispute – whether miracles happen in real time or were programmed into creation[16] – reflects other disagreements about the processes of creation and the nature of Divine Providence. The majority opinion perceives the laws of nature as the primary expression of Hashem's hand in the world, and therefore any deviation from those laws detracts, so to speak, from Hashem's greatness. Hashem is "He, who in His goodness, renews the works of creation every day."[17] In effect, the most perfect demonstration of Hashem's creative powers included the implantation in creation of all miracles that would be needed throughout history.

What happened here? Another Midrash[18] elaborates that, of the seven natural wonders that have occurred in the world, the miracle at Givon was the sixth. "From creation itself, the sun and the moon acted in concert, neither encroaching on the other, until Yehoshua came, and waged the war of Israel. Then, on Shabbat eve [as the war progressed], he saw the travail of Israel not to desecrate Shabbat… and called out in the name of Hashem that the sun should stand for thirty-six hours until Shabbat ended," enabling Israel to complete the battle.

Thus, there is a second reason why the miracle was imperative: to avoid a desecration of Shabbat. Certainly, Jewish life could be preserved through warfare on Shabbat, but Yehoshua was unsure whether Shabbat could be

---

15. Midrash Breisheet Raba 6:9.
16. A discussion is found in Rambam's *Moreh Nevuchim*, Part 2, Chapter 29.
17. From the daily *Shacharit* prayers, the first blessing preceding *Kriat Shema*.
18. Midrash Pirkei D'Rabbi Eliezer, Chapter 51.

desecrated to save the Givonim. He prayed for the miracle, in essence, to avoid the *halachic* question.

The Gemara (Avoda Zara 25a) records three opinions regarding the nature and extent of the miracle. "Rav Yehoshua ben Levi held that the miracle lasted for twenty-four hours in total, and the sun would alternately stand and move every six hours. Rav Eliezer maintained (like the Midrash above) that the sun, twice, moved for six hours and stood for twelve hours – so in fact the miracle itself extended for thirty-six hours. Rav Shmuel bar Nachmani concluded that the complete miracle continued over forty-eight hours.[19] In effect, the sun stood – in stages - in order to prolong Friday, and delay the onset of Shabbat until the battle was over.

Extended daylight over Israel must mean extended nightfall somewhere else, particularly in the Western Hemisphere. Interestingly, such a phenomenon did occur contemporaneous to this event, and was duly recorded in the annals of ancient man – among them the lore of the American Indian, the Hindus, Chinese, Buddhists, and Herodotus's account of old Egyptian chronicles.[20] The Aztec tradition in Mexico notes that in approximately the year 1400 BCE (roughly the time of Yehoshua's conquest of the land of Israel) "the sun failed to rise for a whole day in the City of the Gods, Teotihuacan (north of Mexico City). Likewise, it failed to rise for twenty hours in the Andes, according to Inca legends" of the same period.[21] We do not require independent corroboration of the words of our prophets; it is sufficient that Hashem termed them "prophets of truth whose words are true."[22] But such confirmations are fascinating nonetheless, and are ample testimony to the fact that the nations of the world witnessed this miracle.

In any event, it is clear that the miracle was not a military necessity. Chazal suggested a third reason why the miracle was performed – to enhance and glorify the reputation of Yehoshua among the people of Israel. The Midrash[23] expounds the verse (Tehillim 19:3) "Day following day brings expressions of praise." "What is the character of these two days? The "day" of Moshe heralded the "day" of Yehoshua, for the sun stood still for Moshe

---

19. The Gemara then quotes a Tosefta that has a different configuration of times for each sage.
20. Rav Avigdor Miller, *Behold a People*, page 171.
21. Zecharia Sitchin, letter to the *New York Times*, March 1, 1990.
22. Introductory blessing to the *haftara*.
23. Midrash Yalkut Shimoni, Tehillim, 672.

when he fought Amalek.[24] On that occasion, Moshe prayed that "it should be Your will that the sun should pause for Yehoshua just as it paused for me." When the sun stood still for Yehoshua, his greatness was confirmed in the eyes of all Israel – and in the eyes of the nations of the world who realized that nature itself was on the side of the Jews, and the conquest of Israel was therefore inevitable.

"Is this not written in the *Book of the Upright*?" (Yehoshua 10:13). Radak writes that this refers to the Torah, and substantiated what Hashem had said to Moshe in the aftermath of the sin of the golden calf: "Behold, I make a covenant: before your entire people I shall make wonders such as have never been created in the entire world and before all the nations, and the entire people among whom you are will see the work of Hashem – which is awesome – that I am about to do with you" (Shemot 34:10). The two wonders were the radiance of Moshe's face and the sun at Givon.[25]

Malbim[26] adds that the "wonders" that Hashem promised were distinguished in three ways: they would take place in front of the entire nation, were unprecedented in kind, and renowned throughout the world – so the entire world would know of Hashem's special relationship with the Jewish people. This covenant was fulfilled here at Givon. More importantly, after this covenant the Torah immediately admonished the Jewish people to make no treaties with the indigenous population, for Hashem will drive them out of the land (Shemot 34:11–12). In other words, the promise of the conquest of the land was inextricably linked to the promise of the performance of miracles and wonders during that very conquest.

Rashi[27] traces this aggrandizement of Yehoshua's name to Yaakov's blessing of his grandson Efraim, the ancestor of Yehoshua: "…and his offspring's fame will fill the nations" (Breisheet 49:19). Accordingly, the

---

24. The Gemara Avoda Zara (25a) states that the sun stood still when Moshe fought the Emori. This miracle was not publicized in the Torah, as many of Moshe's miracles were not. It was known to the people, so when Yehoshua stopped the sun, it invited a favorable comparison with Moshe. See further for another reason why Moshe's miracle of the sun was not explicitly recognized in the Torah.
25. Radak, Yehoshua 10:12, quoting his father. Ralbag here argues that the "*Book of the Upright*" was a chronicle of the history of Israel that was lost when we were exiled. The Gemara (Avoda Zara 25a) offers several other possibilities.
26. Malbim, Yehoshua 10:12–13.
27. Rashi, Yehoshua 10:13.

miracle at Givon consolidated Yehoshua's leadership, and raised his esteem among the people.

Abravanel offers a fourth reason for the miracle – to glorify Hashem before the people and the nations. "Usually, Hashem will only perform a miracle if physically necessary, or if it will provide some intellectual or moral perfection to the witnesses. This miracle at Givon conveyed to the Jewish people a certain knowledge of the true faith – that Hashem is the Creator and Master of the universe."[28]

Bear in mind that the people who entered Israel were primarily not the same people who experienced the miracles in Egypt and had grown accustomed to the desert *mon* (manna) and the wells of water, without necessarily appreciating their divine origin. They did not witness any special miracles during their sojourn in the wilderness, only the deaths of their older contemporaries. They had witnessed Hashem's mastery of the water (splitting the Jordan River) and His control over the land (the tumbling of the walls of Yericho), but not Hashem's supremacy over the heavens. The miracle at Givon affirmed that idea as well, and this event reinforced the Jewish people's relationship with Hashem and our awareness of His nature. In a short time, they experienced the variety of miracles that their predecessors had witnessed in Egypt and Sinai, "in order that you will know that I am Hashem in the midst of the land" (Shemot 8:18).

This miracle was also unique in that all other miracles came about through Hashem's will or at the initiative of a prophet; here, Yehoshua himself decreed that the wonder occur. All other miracles exalt God's name or save Israel from some distress; here, Israel was already saved, and the miracle testified to Hashem's continued direction of our destiny. Thus, "there was no day like that before it or after it, that Hashem listened to the voice of a man, that Hashem did battle for Israel" (Yehoshua 10:15).[29] Such a miracle reinforced in the national identity of Israel a special, deep bond with Hashem, a historical memory that would endure for the ages. And never before or since did a human being pray to Hashem for a supernatural occurrence and have Hashem respond immediately.[30]

---

28. Abravanel, Yehoshua 10.
29. Malbim, Yehoshua 10:15.
30. Radak, Yehoshua 10:14. Moshe, though, was able to perform miracles on his own. (See the esoteric comments of Avraham ibn Ezra, Bamidbar 20:8.)

There is a fifth reason as well for the occurrence of the miracle. Rashi[31] commented on two anomalies in verse 12: the beginning "*Az yedaber Yehoshua la'Hashem,*" then Yehoshua spoke to God, which clearly evokes Moshe's song at the sea ("*Az yashir Moshe…,*" then Moshe sang [Shemot 15:10]), and "*shemesh b'Givon dom,*" sun in Givon, stand still. "*Dom*" literally means "be silent"; the Hebrew word for "stand still" would be "*amod.*" What is the reference to *shira*, and to the silence of the sun?

Rashi explains: "Yehoshua had to offer a song in place of the sun, because the sun was temporarily silenced from uttering its song to Hashem. As long as the sun cannot sing, it cannot move; for as long as it moves, it sings."[32] The sun – all of nature – sings to Hashem, in the sense that the exquisite natural order testifies to the harmony of creation and the majesty of the Creator. This is the focus of our monthly *kiddush levana* (the blessing of the new moon). The moon is the only entity in creation that changes in size and shape before our eyes, and therefore reminds us of Hashem's creative powers. All of nature remains unchanged to our eyes; only the moon appears different on a daily basis as it passes through the lunar cycle. This is one song of creation.

There is a more abstruse song, as well, that is difficult to fully comprehend. Rambam[33] states that "the stars and the spheres have a soul and intelligence and they acknowledge the Creator, each one according to its greatness and level praises God just like the angels. The intelligence of the stars is lesser than that of the angels, but greater than that of human beings." What does this mean? The simplest explanation is that there is a realm of intelligence that is beyond ours, and that we cannot fully understand. We are aware of the existence of this level of knowledge, but its substance is beyond our perception. We perceive the luminaries as inanimate, but on a level of knowledge that exceeds our own and in a mode of communication that transcends ours, the luminaries offer their own undiluted, uncorrupted praise of Hashem that is more coherent than man's praise.

Then by what right did Yehoshua interfere with the song of the sun? We have offered technical reasons: so the Emori should not escape in the darkness of night,[34] or to prevent injury to the Jewish soldiers who would

---

31. Rashi, Yehoshua 10:12.
32. Reminiscent of Tehillim 19:2, "the heavens relate the glory of God."
33. Rambam, Hilchot Yesodei HaTorah 3:9.
34. *Metzudot David*, Yehoshua 10:12.

otherwise pursue the Emori at night.³⁵ There is a more profound reason that induced Yehoshua to change the course of nature. Yehoshua did not merely interrupt the sun's song; he was attempting to supplant it. He was articulating our vision of the world, that those creatures who use their free choice to obey God's will are on a higher level than those entities that sing God's praises but are not free to dissent. The sun may have greater "intelligence" (in the language of the Rambam) and sing a more sublime song than man, but it cannot be a greater servant of God than man is. That distinction rests with human beings who must subdue their inclinations and choose to obey the Torah, not with the created entities that have no free choice and simply follow Hashem's will, and "cannot deviate from their assigned tasks."³⁶

At this climactic battle for the land of Israel, Yehoshua introduced a profound concept that the people should always contemplate: the Jewish people, as a nation, stand in the universe in a more influential position even than the sun. We have the capacity to inculcate in mankind the idea of God, and praise of God, in a way that they can accept and appreciate. The heavenly bodies cannot do that, and so in service of God and in propagating God's message to mankind, they are inferior to us. The miracle was not necessary to win the war, and there might have been other ways to enhance Yehoshua's reputation and standing; the miracle was indispensable on a spiritual level, to remind the Jewish people of our divine mission.

We only refer to the song of nature,³⁷ but we attempt to imitate the song of the angels. Our *kedusha* prayer is lifted verbatim from the angels.³⁸ We try to copy both their words and their physical deportment. But only *our* praise of God can supersede that of the angels and the rest of creation, because man must undergo a process of self-perfection in order to be worthy to sing this song.

Yehoshua's song, albeit exceedingly brief, was one of the ten songs in the Bible,³⁹ and emulated Moshe's song at the sea – another divine intervention with a natural body. The fundamental song of God's world is chanted

---

35. Abravanel, Yehoshua 10:12.
36. From the Birkat Levana.
37. As in Tehillim 19.
38. The text of *kedusha* begins "We will sanctify Your name in this world, just as they sanctify You in the heavens…"
39. Targum, on Shir Hashirim 1:1.

not by the angels but by mortal, frail, imperfect man – who, despite his flaws, always has the potential to be called "a man of God."[40] It is the song that animates our lives, shapes our destiny, and awaits our enthusiastic chorus. Through the Torah, the *mitzvot,* and the land of Israel, we harmonize all of creation and bring God's song to the world. The *Az yedaber* ("then he will speak") of Yehoshua surely evokes the *Az yashir* ("then he will sing") as a song of the future, not only the past.[41]

Aftermath

The five kings fled to Makkedah where they were cornered in a cave, in today's Valley of Elah. Yehoshua returned to Gilgal, but sent a small force to guard that cave. Soon, the kings emerged, were captured and hanged, and their bodies were returned to their cave. Resistance collapsed, and the conquest of the land of Israel proceeded without impediment. Yehoshua triumphantly marched through the land of Israel, conquering the southern cities of Israel – Hevron, Lachish and others – except for Yerushalayim, which was left for King David to vanquish several centuries later.

The miracle of the sun standing still introduced a new dynamic in Jewish life – the unity of the miraculous and the natural, collaborating to achieve a common goal. Previously, miracles and nature operated sequentially. In Yericho, for example, the walls collapsed miraculously, and then the Jews walked in and destroyed the city. In Ai, the city was conquered naturally according to Hashem's word, and then the miracle occurred. Here, the Jews fought with the sword, aided by hail from Above, and the sun and the moon subordinated themselves to the goals of Hashem's cherished servants. Heaven and earth were unified, which is the ultimate fulfillment of our role in mankind.

Until now, Hashem fought our battles and we were passive, or we fought the battles and Hashem assisted behind the scenes. Even in Moshe's wars, there was no coupling of the miraculous and the natural; that was purely an *Eretz Yisrael* phenomenon. That is why the Torah never refers to Moshe's miracle of the sun; the time was not ripe for such concerted powers to become part of our arsenal. Here, at Givon, the two forces acted in concert – the Jews fighting naturally and Hashem simultaneously produc-

---

40. Devarim 33:1, in reference to Moshe.
41. Rashi, Shemot 15:1.

ing supernatural occurrences, a two-pronged attack that left our enemies depleted and despondent. This was unique to our conquest of the land, and this miracle therefore was part of Yehoshua's (and not Moshe's) identity.

For the Jewish people, it was a reflection of our destiny and the achievement of "I fashioned this people for Myself, that it might declare My praise" (Yeshayahu 43:21). Hashem created us for a purpose: to sing His praises. We sing His praises most when we successfully harmonize the physical and spiritual worlds, the miraculous and the natural. This is the sanctification of Hashem's name that is the mandate and mission of the Jewish people, and the special responsibility of those who revitalize Jewish national life in the land of Israel.

Often, we lose our true national identity in the thicket of politics, diplomacy, international intrigue and military exploits. Those are important, but subordinate, aspects of modern Jewish life, certainly far less significant than an awareness of our place in history and in the destiny of the Jewish people. We fail to recognize the historic times in which we live, and underrate events of cosmic significance – the return to Israel, the ingathering of the exiles – which have occurred before our eyes. The natural blends with the supernatural, and effects the salvation according to His will.

Summary

The miracle at Givon exalted Hashem and Yehoshua in the eyes of Israel and the nations, and demonstrated that nature – rather than being all-powerful – is actually the tool of the righteous in their service of Hashem. The natural and the supernatural will join forces to protect Israel when we are worthy.

~(Chapter Eight
YEHOSHUA AND CALEV

THE DOMINANT THEME of the Book of Yehoshua is the division of the land of Israel among the tribes of Israel. Although the land was not completely conquered by Yehoshua – and would not be completely conquered for centuries – Yehoshua, at Hashem's command, undertook the distribution of territories as his last major task.

"Yehoshua was old, advanced in years, and Hashem said to him, 'You have grown old, advanced in years, and very much land remains to be conquered'" (Yehoshua 13:1). And the Navi lists the substantial tracts still to be occupied by Israel. Nevertheless, Hashem said, "And now divide this land as a heritage for the nine tribes, and half the tribe of Menashe" (13:5)[1] – even though the conquest was incomplete. Essentially, it became the responsibility of each tribe to conquer the territory apportioned to it if it still remained in the possession of Canaanites. But why didn't Yehoshua just conquer the entire land, and then divide it?

Rambam[2] explains that *Eretz Yisrael* is defined as any land conquered by a king or prophet of Israel, and such is called a "public conquest" to which the *mitzvot hatluyot ba'aretz*, the laws dependent on residence in the land of Israel, would apply. This is in contrast to a "private conquest," the acquisition of an individual person or tribe, to which the relevant

1. The tribes of Reuven and Gad and the other half of the tribe of Menashe were granted their land in Transjordan (Yehoshua 13:15–32), as they had requested from Moshe (Bamidbar, Chapter 32).
2. Rambam, *Hilchot Terumot* 1:2.

laws of *Eretz Yisrael* would not apply. "For this reason Yehoshua and his tribunal allocated *Eretz Yisrael* to the tribes before the land was fully subjugated – so its later conquest by each tribe should not be construed as a private conquest." For some reason, Yehoshua did not or could not conquer the land in its entirety, and it was left to the tribes to liberate each part of *Eretz Yisrael*.

The land was divided by lottery according to the decisions of the *Urim v'Tumim*[3] – except for the city of Hevron, which was specially allocated to Calev ben Yefuneh, Yehoshua's comrade and fellow survivor of the debacle of the spies and the wilderness experience. Hevron was the very first distribution in the land of Israel and differed from all subsequent distributions: It was made based on a special request, did not utilize a lottery or the *Urim v'Tumim*, and was made for private reasons. The questions are: Why? What is the difference between Hevron and the rest of Israel? Why was Hevron presented to Calev? Why did he ask for it, and why was Yehoshua responsive to his request?

Background

"The children of Yehuda approached Yehoshua in Gilgal, and Calev ben Yefuneh the Kenizi[4] said to him, 'you are aware of what Hashem told Moshe concerning me and you in Kadesh-Barnea'" (14:6). It is worthwhile noting that this introduction is an almost verbatim duplication of the introductory words of Parshat Vayigash: "And Yehuda approached [Yosef] and said to him…" (Breisheet 44:18). Here, again, the descendant of Yehuda, Calev, approached the descendant of Yosef, Yehoshua. We will return to the significance of this connection later in this chapter.

Calev then launched into an account of his personal history, which is surprising, if only because Yehoshua was surely familiar with every detail.

> I was forty years old when Moshe, Hashem's servant, sent me from Kadesh-Barnea to spy out the land, and I brought him back a report as was in my heart. My brethren who were with me melted the heart

---

3. Bava Batra 122a.
4. Yefuneh was Calev's father, but Kenaz was Calev's stepfather, who married his mother after Yefuneh's death. Calev is termed "Hakenizi" as a gesture of respect to his stepfather Kenaz.

of the people, but I fulfilled the will of Hashem. Moshe swore on that day saying, 'the land on which you tread your foot will surely be yours as a heritage, and to your children forever, because you fulfilled the will of Hashem.' And now Hashem has kept me alive these forty-five years… and I am eighty-five years old today. I am still as strong today as on the day Moshe dispatched me. As my strength was then, so my strength is now for war – to go out and to come in. So now give me the mountain of which Hashem spoke that day, because you heard on that day that the Anakim (giants) were there and that the cities were large and fortified. Perhaps Hashem will be with me, and I will drive them out, as Hashem has spoken.

Yehoshua blessed him and gave Hevron to Calev the son of Yefuneh as a heritage. Therefore Hevron became the heritage of Calev the son of Yefuneh the Kenizi to this day, because he fulfilled the will of Hashem, God of Israel.[5] (Yehoshua 14:7–14)

Several points stand out from Calev's account, aside from its obviousness to Yehoshua who was present with Calev when each of these events transpired. Calev came with his entire tribe as a show of strength, and a show of unanimous tribal support for this unilateral request. What is astonishing is that Calev completely omitted any mention of Yehoshua's role! "Moshe sent me… I brought back a report… I fulfilled the will of Hashem… Hashem has sustained me until today… I am still as strong as on the day Moshe sent me." What about… "us" or "we"? Yehoshua was an equal partner – perhaps even a senior partner – in their faithful service to Moshe. But Calev spoke as if Yehoshua played no role in the mission of the spies, save for a solitary reference that God said something to Moshe "concerning me and concerning you in Kadesh-Barnea." It is a strange, self-centered formulation (almost like the memoirs of a petty politician) – certainly unexpected from a righteous person like Calev. What message was he conveying to Yehoshua?

Radak[6] references the famous exposition[7] on the verse describing the mission of Moshe's spies: "*They* ascended in the south and *he* arrived at

---

5. In actuality, since Hevron was one of the cities of refuge, it technically belonged to the tribe of Levi. But Calev was given the fields and surrounding lands of Hevron, including the Cave of Machpela, the burial place of our forefathers and foremothers.
6. Radak, Yehoshua, 14:9.
7. Cited by Rashi, Bamidbar 13:22.

Hevron…" (Bamidbar 13:22). Of all the spies, only Calev came to Hevron; the others were terrified of the giants. Calev was courageous, and he alone went to pray at the graves of the Patriarchs. Radak states: "Therefore, Moshe promised the city of Hevron to Calev. And even if this grant was not recorded explicitly in the Torah, it was known to be true, as Calev related it and Yehoshua readily agreed."

But why did Calev go to Hevron? Why didn't Yehoshua go to Hevron – surely he was as intrepid as Calev? And it is even more interesting that the wicked spies used the city of Hevron to bolster their contention that the land of Israel was unconquerable: "But [our attempted conquest] is for naught as the people who dwell in the land are powerful… and we also saw [in Hevron] the offspring of the giant" (Bamidbar 13:28).

The Torah does briefly mention Hashem's promise to Calev: "And my servant Calev, because a different spirit was with him and he followed Me wholeheartedly, I shall bring him *to the land to which he came* and his offspring shall possess it" (Bamidbar 14:24). While Rashi there explicitly refers this promise to the city of Hevron, Ramban notices the absence of any reference to Yehoshua. "Why was Yehoshua's reward neglected? Because it would be unseemly to divulge Yehoshua's reward – the leadership of Israel in place of Moshe."[8] But, in fact, Ramban implies that Calev and Yehoshua were equal in righteousness; in one verse (14:30) Calev is mentioned first, whereas in another verse (14:38) Yehoshua is mentioned first.[9] Both were entitled to a reward, and both received a reward. But why did Calev covet Hevron?

Abravanel[10] writes that Calev wanted Hevron in order to memorialize his fidelity and steadfastness during the sin of the spies. He did not want his righteousness to be forgotten by his descendants, and not because of a misplaced sense of personal pride. There is an important lesson for generations of Jews in Calev's greatness. In essence, Calev was the critical spy, the "swing vote," so to speak, and the one who rescued the honor of the Jewish people. Even though Yehoshua agreed with Calev in contrast to the other spies, the people perceived Yehoshua as Moshe's primary disciple who could be expected to toe the party line – whatever Moshe wanted. But

8. Ramban, Bamidbar 14:24.
9. The deduction that Chazal make elsewhere when Moshe and Aharon are similarly referred to is that they too were equal. See Rashi, Shemot 6:26.
10. Abravanel, Yehoshua 14:14.

if Yehoshua had been alone in his views, against the opinion of the eleven other, more independent minded, spies, Yehoshua's views would have been discounted altogether.

Calev was therefore a more important figure than Yehoshua in this calamity; but for Calev, the people would have concluded that Moshe cannot be trusted, and a worse disaster – perhaps even a more severe punishment – would have ensued. Calev broke ranks with the other spies, and with his "different spirit" salvaged what he could. He even pretended to agree with part of the spies' report in order to gain the people's attention.[11] This distinction deserved an eternal commemoration, and this motivated Calev's request for the city of Hevron. Its association with Calev reminds us until today – and especially today – that the majority can be wrong (certainly when it adopts a non-Torah and non-nationalist stance) and a small minority can be right, that public opinion is fickle and often ill-conceived, and that decisions that affect the destiny of Israel cannot be entrusted to those who lack a true Torah perspective on the historic mission of Israel and the process of redemption.

Rav Avraham Yitzchak HaKohen Kook commented on the verse: "…with their own eyes they will see that Hashem returns to Zion" (Yeshayahu 52:8)[12] that the phrase "with their own eyes" literally states *"ayin b'ayin,"* the "eye within the eye" will see that Hashem returns to Zion. One cannot uncover or understand the redemptive process with a regular eye; it demands the "eye within the eye," a perception that penetrates beyond the superficial and the transparent. Those who possess this enhanced vision are the natural leaders of Israel. That was Calev's legacy, and that is the heritage of the city of Hevron until today.

Calev and the Monarchy

Certainly, there is more to this story than the conveyance of a certain parcel of land to Calev, however hallowed that land is. Earlier it was noted that Calev's approach to Yehoshua is linguistically (if not thematically) similar to Yehuda's advance to Yosef, the viceroy of Egypt, when Yehuda pleaded for clemency on behalf of his youngest brother, Binyamin. Calev was a scion of

---

11. Rashi, Bamidbar 13:30.
12. *"Ki ayin b'ayin yiru b'shuv Hashem tzion." Torat Eretz Yisrael* by Rabbi David Samson, page 151, cites this comment in the name of Rav Tzvi Yehuda HaKohen Kook.

the tribe of Yehuda, the tribe of monarchy, a privilege bestowed on Yehuda by Yaakov.[13] But the royal prerogatives were not yet ready to be actualized throughout the long sojourn in Egypt and the wilderness; the assertion of kingship by the tribe of Yehuda – and its natural leader, Calev – awaited entry into the land of Israel.

Thus, there is another dynamic in progress here in this dialogue concerning the city of Hevron: Yehuda's claims to the monarchy are awakening, and Calev subtly, respectfully but firmly, informed Yehoshua that, by rights, Calev should rule – and not Yehoshua. That is the inevitable result of the conquest and settlement of the land. Calev therefore emphasized *his* role in disputing the spies, and brought along his entire tribe to stake their claim to the monarchy.

Calev and his tribe made a very powerful and cogent argument. Yehoshua, in fact, had received a reward for his role in the debacle of the spies – the leadership of the Jewish people as they entered and conquered the land of Israel. He himself would have no sons, and therefore not share a physical inheritance in the land.[14] He was "*old, advanced in years*" (13:1), a fact that the Navi concedes. Yehoshua would admittedly not succeed in conquering the entire land of Israel. He could no longer fight or wage war. By contrast, Calev was vigorous, "*still as strong today as I was on the day Moshe sent me… as my strength was then, so is my strength now for war*" (14:11).[15] Yehoshua was old and tired (he was 103 at the time), while Calev was ready, willing and able (relatively young at 85). Apparently, beneath the surface of their dialogue, Calev was asking for more than territory – *he was obliquely asking Yehoshua to abdicate* so Calev and his tribe could assume their natural place at the helm of the ship of state. Yehoshua, in essence, could perform one last act of true and honorable leadership by confirming for the entire nation the monarchy of the tribe of Yehuda.

Furthermore, Yehoshua clearly had shied away from conquering

---

13. Breisheet 49:8–10.
14. Ramban, Bamidbar 14:24, cited in *Mishbetzot Zahav*, page 233.
15. Radak (ibid.) explains that Calev asserted that he was in the best possible position in life – physically, he was as robust as ever, and spiritually, he was "*eighty-five years old*" and beyond the age of temptation. Calev recognized that this was a providential gift, as usually one's physical drives waned along with one's physical abilities. This uniqueness made his request for leadership all the more compelling. (*Mishbetzot Zahav*, page 230.)

Hevron – a most difficult city to conquer because of its hilly terrain.[16] To Calev, this was a repetition of the fears of the spies, who were petrified by what they saw in Hevron. Calev asked for Hevron, and declared that he would conquer it if Yehoshua could not or would not.

Calev had visited Hevron the first time, not only to pray at the graves of our ancestors, but especially to confirm in the minds of the people that our connection to the land of Israel is based on the *Avot*. Hashem's covenant with our forefathers Avraham, Yitzchak and Yaakov gave us our title to the land. Calev wished to substantiate for all time that our title to the land is rooted in our possession of Hevron; if Hevron were to be allotted via a lottery, it would be tantamount to stating that Hevron is territory like all other territory, without any special dimension. But if Hevron is set aside and conveyed in a manner different from all other places in Israel – because it is the *Ir HaAvot*, the city of our fathers, then it accentuates the notion that it is Hashem's covenant with our fathers that gave us our rights to the land. Absent an acknowledgment of Hashem's covenant with our fathers, our rights to the land of Israel are deficient. The city of Hevron links Hashem, the *Avot* and the Jewish people to the land of Israel.[17]

The Jew who wants to possess the land of Israel must recognize the eternal significance of Hevron. It is not the land itself, but the place, where Avraham was circumcised, where the *Avot* dwelled, and where the covenant was confirmed and reconfirmed with each of our fathers.

Calev thus had three contentions. He would lead and conquer, he would exhibit the indefatigability that conquest of the land of Israel requires, and he would reinforce the connection with the *Avot* through possession of the city of Hevron.

If Yehoshua was weary, then Calev was available to step in and lead. If Yehoshua cannot carry on with the conquest of Israel, especially to capture the city of our fathers, then Calev would. It is not uncommon – surely it

---

16. In 1967, for example, the Arabs of Hevron surrendered without a fight, so the Israeli Army did not have to actually conquer the city house-to-house. The hills that surround Hevron offer the occupier a formidable advantage.
17. *Mishbetzot Zahav*, pages 231–232. That is why when, centuries later, the monarchy of Israel was established in its ideal form, King David first ruled for seven years in Hevron. This connection was reinforced every morning in the Bet HaMikdash when the *kohen* in charge asked: "Is the eastern sky bright? Even to Hevron?" in order to cite the merit of our fathers. (Yoma 28a; Yerushalmi Yoma 3:1.)

has become quite common in recent years – for elderly leaders to tire in office, abandon their lifelong, cherished values and embrace the policies of their lifelong opponents.[18]

Calev stated he would stay the course and see the mission to its conclusion. Calev also asserted that he had one last mission to perform, in a sense a continuation of his role in the wilderness. Then, Calev was a symbol of self-sacrifice, the only one of the spies who was unafraid of entering Hevron, the city of giants. Calev could set an example for generations of Jews. Perhaps there would come a time when Jews would again be afraid of conquering the land, or afraid of entering or visiting different parts of the land of Israel; if so, Calev could then serve as the symbol of perseverance, fearlessness and valor for all time. And, to fortify our claim to the land through the *Avot*, Calev emphasized that the city of Hevron must have a unique status when *Eretz Yisrael* is divided among the tribes.

What emerged here was another manifestation of the struggle between the sons of Leah and the sons of Rachel, which first arose in Parshat Vayetzei (Breisheet, Chapter 30) and erupted in the strife between Yosef and his brothers, and the confrontation of Yehuda and Yosef mentioned above. Once again, the offspring of Leah – Calev – asserted his prerogatives against the offspring of Rachel – Yehoshua.[19] Again, as would happen when Shaul preceded David as king of Israel, the scion of Rachel (Yehoshua) ruled first, and, here, instead of the descendant of Leah (Calev). The vision of Yechezkel – the reunification of Yehuda and Efraim – was still millennia away. Why does Jewish history unfold in this manner?

Yehoshua was the second leader of Israel, but, in a sense, the first native, homegrown leader.[20] Moshe, to all intents and purposes, had been raised outside the family of Israel – first in the palace of Pharaoh, and then as a fugitive for over six decades. Moshe returned to the Jewish people at the advanced age of eighty, and, not coincidentally, Moshe's leadership

18. Ariel Sharon, whose political career emphasized building settlements and who as prime minister has dismantled and destroyed them, is just the latest example.
19. It would continue in the rivalry of Shaul and David, in the division of the Jewish people into the dueling monarchies of Yehuda and Yisrael (Efraim), and the ultimate emergence of Moshiach ben Yosef and then Moshiach ben David. The rift will only be fully healed in the Messianic era, as prophesied by Yechezkel (37:15–28), the *haftara* of *Parshat Vayigash*, when Hashem "will make them into a single nation… and they will no longer be two nations, no longer divided into two kingdoms (ibid. 37:22).
20. Based on *Me'avoor Ha'aretz*, pages 154–155.

was constantly challenged – by Datan and Aviram, Korach, the spies, and various groups among the people. On some level, he was perceived as never having suffered in Egypt as did everyone else, and so was never fully embraced by the people. It might indeed have been one of the causes of Moshe's initial reluctance to assume the position as leader of Israel.[21]

By contrast, Yehoshua was never challenged – until now – and even this showdown was implied, rather than direct, and respectful in tone. Yehoshua had been enslaved in Egypt along with the others, and his governance was appreciated. That is not to say that he was universally beloved – no Jewish leader has ever merited that, nor ever will. One of the arguments raised by Achan in defense of his misappropriation of property was that, as a descendant of Yehuda, Achan was part of the ruling elite and therefore need not obey Yehoshua's edicts. But Achan was obviously wicked, and so his pretensions were not taken seriously. Not so Calev, who was a most admired figure in Israel.

Calev, in fact, used the classic expression of leadership to subtly stake his claim. His strength is undiminished "to go out and to come in" (Yehoshua 14:11), to go out with the people into battle and return with them from battle. He does not stand aloof, issuing orders from a distance. This is a euphemism for leadership, employed by Moshe when he sought a successor "who shall go out before them and come in before them" (Bamidbar 27:17). In these words, familiar to Yehoshua, Calev asked for the reins of leadership.

How did Yehoshua respond to all these challenges? With the greatness that typified him. "And Yehoshua blessed him, and gave Hevron to Calev ben Yefuneh as a heritage" (Yehoshua 14:13). He would not step down, but Hevron would have the unique status that Calev suggested, and Calev himself could conquer and possess it for all generations. Rather than object to Calev's tactics or historical account, Yehoshua embraced it as much as he could and thereby defused a tense situation.

Contrast this with Yehoshua's response to the grievance of his own tribe. After the distribution of the land of Israel, his own tribe of Yosef complained that the lottery apportioned them too little land, and they needed more. "Yehoshua said to them, 'If you are such a numerous people, ascend to the forest and clear an area for yourselves in the land of the Perizi and

---

21. Heard from Rav Sholom Gold of Yerushalayim, Parshat Shemot.

the Refaim… The mountain of Efraim shall be yours because it is a forest. Cut it down and its outskirts will be yours'" (Yehoshua 17:14–18). Yehoshua's tribe sought special treatment; he said, in effect, if you need more land, capture it yourself. Their pleas did not move him at all.

Why was Yehoshua so accommodating to Calev and so grudging to his own tribe? The key to successful leadership is the realization that people are not monolithic, and at times require different treatment. Yehoshua knew how to talk to the Givonim, or the tribe of Yehuda, or Calev, or the tribe of Yosef, or (later) to the daughters of Tzlafchad (Yehoshua 17:3–5), or the tribes that remained in Transjordan. He left most of his interlocutors satisfied, if not fully content, with his decisions. He was a master at human relations. Had Yehoshua been selfishly protective of his command, he would have stonewalled Calev (as only politicians can), stating that elementary fairness demands that there be no special allocations, that the lottery must control, that he must consult the Sanhedrin, etc. Yehoshua chose none of those options, accepted Yehuda's claim to leadership and Calev's claim to Hevron, and even blessed him. He said to Calev, in essence, "the crown is yours; you just cannot wear it while I am alive." Calev acquiesced.

It was a great moment for Calev, as his claim of leadership was accepted, although deferred. In due course, Calev conquered Hevron and environs after enlisting the help of his stepbrother, Otniel ben Kenaz. Otniel was rewarded with Calev's daughter Achsah, as his wife (Yehoshua 15:13–19), and Otniel after Yehoshua's death became the first Judge of Israel. Here, too, the monarchy of Israel followed its natural progression, from the tribe of Yosef to the tribe of Yehuda – already in the generation after Yehoshua and Calev. Otniel was the first representative of the tribe of Yehuda to become the leader of Israel.

Yehoshua, chosen by Hashem,[22] was the ideal leader of Israel for this era. He knew with whom to be firm and with whom to be gentle. Yehoshua understood well his role – as successor to Moshe and conqueror of the land – and his limitations, as a ruler from the tribe of Yosef, and not Yehuda. As such, he never sought to restrain the burgeoning of the tribe of Yehuda. He saw himself – as all leaders from the tribe of Yosef did and would – as a transitional figure. Yosef was himself a transitional ruler, guiding his family from Israel into the Egyptian exile. Similarly, Yehoshua

---

22. Bamidbar 27:18.

shepherded the Jewish people from exile back to the land of Israel. Shaul, the first king (a descendant of Rachel, through Binyamin) was the connective link between the idea of monarchy and the ideal monarch. And Moshiach ben Yosef himself is a transitional leader, who will establish the material infrastructure of the revived land of Israel. The descendants of Yosef always serve a preparatory role for the tribe of Yehuda, laying the groundwork and building the infrastructure for the royal house of Israel. It is possible for the Jewish people to be ruled by temporary figures whose gifts lie in one particular area of nation building, and not another, in order to properly construct the foundations of the state.

Yehoshua acknowledged this, and therefore the Jewish people were spared the leadership conflicts so common among the nations of the world when a new state is born – who will be the first leader, and who will be his successor. Often, even if the leader of the revolution has widespread acceptance, a major (usually violent) struggle will erupt over the choice of his successor (if there is a "choice"), the "keeper of the flame." We were saved from that strife because of the greatness of Yehoshua who accepted that the sons of Leah and the sons of Rachel will always be rival factions in the Jewish people, with different roles, strengths and weaknesses – but each indispensable to our national mission. Until the reunification occurs at the end of days, the Jewish leader must be able to finesse the various interests, competing factions and sundry agendas that constitute the people of Israel.

When the leader fails to do that, as in the split that took place in the generation after the reign of King Shlomo, the Jewish people divided into two warring groups and the achievement of our destiny was thwarted.

In modern times, the leaders of Israel have almost always focused on material issues – conquest, defense, security, economics – and the fundamental questions of Jewish identity, the meaning and substance of a Jewish state, and the incorporation of Torah law and ethics into that state – have been deferred. Such a postponement is natural when confronted with real and persistent threats to one's very existence, but it comes at a cost. The reluctance to accept or articulate the uniqueness of Jewish nationhood deprives many people of the passionate bond to Torah, *Klal Yisrael* and *Eretz Yisrael* they might otherwise have had, and has a harmful strategic dimension. It saps the will of the people in the face of the relentless hostility of the enemy, as they lack answers to the profound existential questions of our time: for what exactly are they fighting? Israel is a refuge for the Jewish people, but a refuge for what purpose? Why is it necessary, or even important, that the Jewish people survive?

Transitional leaders or uni-dimensional leaders, who may themselves lack a clear understanding of these issues, are ill-equipped to offer proper guidance. That becomes the natural role of the Torah authorities; yet, because in Israel they have often been perceived as tangential to the affairs of state – and have often intentionally made themselves tangential to the affairs of state by declining to participate fully in state building or national defense – they have been unfortunately relegated to the sidelines. There has been, recently, some gradual change, as recognition of the dangers of an ambiguous national identity has grown, and there must be further change until the leadership of the Jewish people embraces the ideals of Torah as national policy, and perceives the Torah not as "ritual law" but as the constitution and foundation of the Jewish people. Indeed, Moshiach is characterized as "a scion of the House of David, who meditates in Torah and is involved in *mitzvot* like David, who [through the force of his personality] compels Torah observance, and fights Hashem's battles. Such a leader is presumed to be the Messiah, and if he builds the *Bet HaMikdash* and gathers the exiles, he is certainly the Messiah."[23]

The true Jewish leader, therefore, synthesizes the spiritual, political, and material aspects of Jewish national life – without any dichotomy, embarrassment or inner contradiction. He is a leader who recognizes the continuity of Jewish life – from the *Avot* to Sinai to today – and sees his nation as heirs to Hashem's covenant with our forefathers. He perceives his mission as magnifying the name of Hashem and His Torah among the Jewish people and the world. We await that leader eagerly, and desperately.

One of the goals of Yehoshua's leadership was the ratification of Yehuda as the royal house of Israel, and the acknowledgment that he, Yehoshua, was but a temporary steward – at Hashem's bidding – of the government of Israel. He relinquished power quite readily and did not seek to choose his successor. He averted a struggle over succession, even if the period of the Shoftim (Judges) would be marked by inconsistent leadership and social chaos. The nation knew they were biding their time until the foundation of Jewish monarchy would be laid.

---

23. Rambam, Hilchot Melachim 11:4.

The rapprochement between Calev and Yehoshua cemented the framework of leadership in Israel and the orderly transition of power. It confirmed for all time two basic principles of Jewish life that guide us until today, aside from the allotment of the land of Israel: the tribe of Yehuda as the natural leaders of Israel, and our connection to the land as grounded in the covenant with the *Avot*.

The granting of Hevron to Calev – and all that implied – was, in essence, Yehoshua's final decision as leader.[24] It is therefore his legacy and an everlasting expression of his greatness, as it precluded a leadership struggle, reinforced the political norms of the Torah and kept the people focused on the goal of building the land of Israel as a kingdom of priests and a holy nation.

Summary

The special conveyance of the city of Hevron to Calev highlighted the covenant with the *Avot* as our true title to the land, and substantiated the royal claims of the house of Yehuda. It is a reminder that the Jewish people can be governed by transitional leaders who focus on conquest and the material construction of the land, while awaiting the permanent Torah leaders who synthesize the material and the spiritual and consecrate all aspects of the land of Israel to service of God.

---

24. The distribution of land took place through a lottery and was not completely under Yehoshua's control. See next chapter.

Chapter Nine
THE DIVISION OF THE LAND

THE DIVISION OF THE LAND of Israel was the culmination of events dating back to the time of Avraham. It was one of the goals of the Exodus from Egypt, and the fulfillment of the fundamental covenant between Hashem and our forefathers, "for all the land you see, to you and your descendants will I give it forever" (Breisheet 13:15).[1] The distribution was the essential purpose of the Book of Yehoshua. "Rav Ada the son of Rabbi Chanina stated: 'If the Jewish people had not sinned, they only would have been given the Five Books of the Torah *and the Book of Yehoshua*, the latter because it teaches the disposition (literally, the arrangement) of the land of Israel.'"[2] The Torah provided us with the *mitzvot*, and the Book of Yehoshua imparted to us the arrangements of the various plots of land among the tribes, and the value of the land of Israel conceptually.[3] The other books of the prophets and the Ketuvim (Writings) deal largely with sin, sinners and the aftermath of sin – admonitions, warnings, threats, punishments, exhortations and repentance.

The allocation of land occurred over the course of seven years, and spans more than ten chapters in Yehoshua. And yet, the seven years of conquest and the seven years of distribution[4] did not result in the acquisition

---

1. This covenant to Avraham was renewed to Yitzchak (Breisheet 26:3) and to Yaakov (Breisheet 28:13 and 35:12).
2. Masechet Nedarim 22b.
3. Rashi, ibid.
4. Masechet Arachin 13a.

of the entire land of Israel as promised in the Torah. The covenant with Avraham delineated the Promised Land as stretching "from the River of Egypt[5] to the great river, the Euphrates" (Breisheet 15:18). This was reiterated later in Moshe's time: "Wherever you trod your feet, that land shall be yours – from the Wilderness and the Lebanon, from the River Euphrates until the Western Sea[6] shall be your boundary" (Devarim 11:24). The Biblical borders of Israel therefore extend to modern day Iraq, Lebanon, Syria and Egypt, surely disheartening news to those countries – some of which use this knowledge to ascribe nefarious intentions to the modern State of Israel. They need not fear; the *Tevuot Ha'aretz* comments that Israel's extended borders, as the Torah prescribes, will only apply when the Jewish people are so numerous that the land of Israel between the Jordan River and the Mediterranean Sea is not large enough to contain us. That has never happened, neither in Yehoshua's time nor in any subsequent era. It has always been unnecessary to conquer land that far east, and it still remains unnecessary. Israel today, in its natural borders from Lebanon to Sinai and from the river to the sea, can more than accommodate all the Jews in the world.

Thus, the Torah may set aside that land – as far as the Euphrates and the River of Egypt – for Jewish settlement, but it is uncertain whether that expansive *Eretz Yisrael* will ever be a national requirement.

How was the land of Israel distributed? What was the method, and how were the tribes all satisfied – such as they were – with their allotments?

The Navi recorded Hashem's directive to Yehoshua: "So now divide this land as a heritage for the nine tribes and half the tribe of Menashe" (Yehoshua 13:7). Reuven, Gad, and the other half of Menashe had already in Moshe's time received their portion on the eastern bank of the Jordan, which was now confirmed by Yehoshua.[7] Even then, not all Jews chose to enter and dwell in the land of Israel, a situation that would recur during the Second Temple era and again in modern times. Yehoshua's task, and that of subsequent leaders down to our day, was to maintain the connection and fidelity of Diaspora Jews to the homeland. He accomplished this by acknowledging their contributions to the conquest of the land and

---

5. Alternately understood as either the Nile River (Targum Yonatan) or Wadi El-Arish (ibn Ezra).
6. The Mediterranean Sea.
7. Yehoshua 13:7–8.

emphasizing the primacy of Torah, which obligates all Jews.[8] Thus, when those tribes built their own altar in Transjordan, the tribes of the land of Israel perceived this as a *casus belli* and mobilized for war.[9] That war was averted only when the tribes of Transjordan explained that they feared the people of Israel would eventually reject them as outsiders who have no share in the Jewish people, deconsecrated their altar, and re-affirmed their allegiance to the people and land of Israel.[10] But the mutual uneasiness remained, and the ties did eventually fray. The tribes in Transjordan would be the first tribes to suffer the fate of exile as the First Temple era neared its conclusion. Today's relationship between the Jews of the Diaspora and the State of Israel – an unequal partnership of unclear parameters – essentially repeats the pattern of ancient times.

Only one tribe was omitted from the distribution: "But to the tribe of Levi, Moshe gave no heritage; Hashem, Lord of Israel is their heritage, as He had spoken to them" (13:33). The *Levi'im* were denied a physical heritage in the land of Israel – and exempted from public or military service – "because they were set apart to serve God, and teach His upright ways and righteous laws to the masses."[11] Thus, as some Jews did not dwell in the land of Israel, others who dwelled in the land focused exclusively on divine service and did not fully participate in the mundane aspects of life. Both phenomena exist today as well and remain a source of great controversy and debate.

The method of allotment had already been pronounced by Hashem to Moshe: "To these shall the land be divided as an inheritance, according to the number of names. For the numerous one, you shall increase its inheritance; and for the lesser one, you shall decrease its inheritance. Each one according to his count shall his inheritance be given. *Only by lottery shall the land be divided, according to the names of their fathers' tribes shall they inherit.* According to the lottery shall one's inheritance be divided, between the numerous and the few" (Bamidbar 26:52–56). The Torah states unequivocally that the lottery – *goral* – would determine the distribution.

Chazal maintain that an additional method was employed – the *Urim v'Tumim*.[12] But how is it possible to assert that the *Urim v'Tumim* were

---

8. Ibid 22: 1–8.
9. Ibid 22:12.
10. Ibid 22:21–29.
11. Rambam, Mishna Torah, Laws of Shmita and Yovel 13:12–13.
12. Masechet Bava Batra 122a. The *Urim v'Tumim* were a form of divine communication (a

used, when the Torah states clearly that a lottery was used? In the words of the Rashbam[13]: "If you have the *Urim v'Tumim*, why do you need the lottery? And if you have the lottery, why use the *Urim v'Tumim*? Perhaps they might even contradict each other!"

The Gemara explains the process: Elazar the *kohen gadol* wore the *Urim v'Tumim*, and Yehoshua and all of Israel stood before him, along with two containers of cards. One container held the names of the tribes, and the other contained the names of the various territories to be dispensed among the tribes. Yehoshua, with divine inspiration, would pronounce, for example, "Zevulun, ascend!", the *Urim v'Tumim* would spell out Zevulun's name, and the *Urim v'Tumim* would then flash "Akko region." This was done for every tribe, respectively. Then, after the prophecy of the *Urim v'Tumim*, each tribal leader[14] would reach into the container, shuffle the cards, and astoundingly pull out the name of his own tribe, say, Zevulun, reach into the other box, shuffle those cards, and amazingly extract the "Akko region" card.[15] The process was then repeated for each tribe. In effect, each selection and distribution was ratified twice before the eyes of the entire nation – once through the *Urim v'Tumim* and once through the lottery – so grievances would be impossible (or at least minimized). People witnessed the hand of Hashem in the apportionment of the land of Israel. With this, Rashbam writes, "Israel was satisfied" with the outcome.

The *Urim v'Tumim per se* would not have been sufficient to assuage the people's concerns, because, as noted, there was an element of arbitrariness in their interpretation. The interpreter, who asked the question, had to arrange the revealed letters in an order that cogently answered his question. But the reply was not disclosed in a way that the average person was able to read and understand it. Conversely, if the only method of distribution was the lottery (a random drawing), aggrieved parties (e.g., those awarded the

lower level than prophecy), which was utilized most often when questions of national import had to be resolved. The *kohen gadol*'s breastplate contained stones on which were inscribed the names of the tribes of Israel. When an appropriate question was asked in the presence of the *kohen gadol*, the letters on the stones of the breastplate would illuminate, and indirectly convey the answer to the questioner, who was required to interpret those letters in order to ascertain the complete answer to his question.

13. Ibid.
14. So says Rashi, Bamidbar 26:54. The Gemara Bava Batra 122a implies that Elazar directed the entire process.
15. Bava Batra 122a, with commentary of Rashbam, and Rashi, Bamidbar 26:54.

Negev desert as opposed to the Sharon Valley) would never be dissuaded that the results were fixed and prearranged by Yehoshua. This dual system, orchestrated by *Ruach HaKodesh*, the Divine Spirit,[16] convinced the people that the results were precisely as ordained in Heaven.

The real issue that concerned the people, as was predictable, was the relative size and value of each tract of land.[17] The parcels were not divided equally, but according to a divine formula over which Yehoshua presided. The commentators differ on the basic question of whether there was any attempt at "equality" in the division of the land.

Rashi,[18] for example, maintained that the more numerous tribes received larger tracts of territory, and consequently there was not an equal division of land amongst the tribes. Yet, each individual Jew within each tribe – except for the firstborn – received an equal portion of land, so, by definition, the more populous tribes required more territory. Ramban[19] disagreed, and contended that the land of Israel was divided into twelve equal portions, and each tribe received the equivalent amount of land. The subdivision of that land within each tribe, however, differed in size, with an individual member of a more populous tribe receiving less land than an individual member of a less populous tribe.

These two opinions reflect the two sides of the dispute brought down in the Gemara Bava Batra (121b–122a): Was the land divided according to the number of tribes (twelve equal shares) or according to the number of heads (equal shares *per capita*)? Strangely, the Gemara concludes that the land was divided equally among the tribes – the opinion of Ramban. How then can Rashi maintain that the equality was for each individual beneficiary, and not for each tribe?

Several resolutions are possible. Certainly, quantity is not the only

---

16. *Ruach HaKodesh* is itself a means of prophecy, similar to the *Urim v'Tumim* (Rambam, Moreh Nevuchim, Part 2, Chapter 45).
17. There are several maps that purport to delineate the division of the land, but these are all approximations. It is not known with any certainty where each city named in the Book of Yehoshua was actually located. Yet, since the general areas are known, towns and cities in Israel today bearing Biblical names are located in the general vicinity of their ancient predecessors. Of course, the location of certain cities is well established (Yerushalayim, Hevron, et al.), as they have had uninterrupted Jewish residence for several millennia.
18. Rashi, Bamidbar 26:54.
19. Ramban, ibid.

method of measuring equality; in Israel – especially in Israel – one must account for the varying quality of the land. As the Gemara (Bava Batra 122a) states: "One *seah* of land in Yehuda is worth five in the Galil." The equitable distribution of land had to account for qualitative differences as well. Israel is unique – perhaps in the world – in the variety of topographies and climates it presents – mountains and valleys, fertile plains and deserts, lush pastures and barren canyons – and all in a geographically small area. A person, if he chose, could ski and swim on the same day in regions that are relatively close to each other. Perhaps, then, the equality of the land for each individual recipient was measured not in size but in value, dependent on objective factors (fertility of the land) and subjective factors (aspirations and interests of the particular tribe).

Malbim[20] adopted the contrasting view of Raavad[21] that the *Urim v'Tumim* and the lottery allocated to the tribes provinces of varying dimensions and attributes. Yehoshua then, with the tribal heads, made territorial adjustments in order to accommodate the needs of the individual tribes and the needs of each recipient family within each tribe. This was done through negotiation, not divine inspiration.

Similarly, Abravanel[22] disagreed with all the other commentators, and argued that parity must consider both quantity and quality, as well as the distinction between lands already conquered and land yet to be conquered. Thus, the provinces allotted to each tribe factored in all these calculations, in order to minimize disputes. After the provinces were distributed, Yehoshua, Elazar and the elders of the tribes determined – subjectively – the final distribution of tracts to each individual family, to further refine the process and produce as equitable a result as was possible. Yehoshua added land to some and subtracted land from others.[23] It is clear, then, how the division of the land consumed a total of seven years.

The one serious complaint lodged against the process came to Yehoshua from his own tribe of Yosef, which resented both the relatively

---

20. Malbim, Yehoshua 14:1.
21. Raavad, as recorded in *Shita Mekubetzet*, Bava Batra 117.
22. Abravanel, Yehoshua, Chapter 14.
23. Pursuant to the principle of *"hefker bet din hefker"* (Yevamot 89b), the Jewish court has full control over the property rights of every Jew, an immense power that the Jewish court can be trusted not to abuse. Ralbag also agrees that Yehoshua prescribed these slight territorial modifications.

small territory given to their populous tribe as well as the allocation to them of primarily unconquered land (Yehoshua 17:14–18). After fourteen years in the land, they had lost their will to fight, preferring, understandably, to settle, build, raise their families, and prosper. To Yehoshua, they addressed only their first issue: "Why have you given me an inheritance of a single lot and a single portion, seeing that I am a numerous people, for Hashem has blessed me to such an extent? …The mountain is insufficient for us, and all the Canaanites that dwell in the land of the valley… have iron chariots" (17:14, 16). In response, Yehoshua addressed only the second – unspoken – issue – the desire to wage war in the land of Israel. "If you are such a numerous people, ascend to the forest and clear an area for yourselves there, in the land of the Perizi and the Refaim… you have great strength… you shall drive out the Canaanites even though they have iron chariots and are strong" (17:15, 17–18).

It was a pointed and timely reminder to his tribe – and, by extension, to all Israel – that the distribution of the land of Israel did not end the conquest or struggle for the land; it was a continuation of the conquest, and the very beginning of the struggle – which, unfortunately, would never end.

The Goals of the Division of the Land

One crucial matter remains for discussion: What was the intent of the distribution of the land? On the surface, it seems like a very prosaic, commonplace political process, analogous, *l'havdil*, to the allocation of territories and drawing of maps by the colonial powers and the League of Nations after World War I, and the similar process undertaken by the United Nations after World War II. For sure, the essential difference was that the distribution of the land of Israel was based on Hashem's wisdom, which guided the entire process. But, on what basis was it determined which tribe would be settled in which province? What were the considerations, such as we can ascertain, that Hashem willed that, for example, the tribe of Zevulun should be granted the province of Akko and the coastal area? The ultimate goal of the settlement of the land of Israel is to implant a holy people on a holy land. How was this desire reflected in the process? And what are the implications for today?

Obviously, the land of Israel was not divided by politicians, diplomats or cartographers but by prophets and Torah Sages - the leading scholars of the generation. That was because the central objective was to ascertain the spiritual essence of each tribe, and to allocate land to each tribe in accordance with each tribe's attributes and spiritual potential. The conquest of the land was not merely a technical act, but the union of the "divine idea" with the "national idea," the full realization of the divine goal to have a holy people living in a particular locale, embracing a unique moral system, and serving as devoted representatives of Hashem and ethical examples to the rest of mankind.[24]

The provision of land was not primarily intended to cater to the economic potential or aspirations of each tribe but rather to their spiritual needs. Yaakov, before his death, "blessed each tribe according to each one's appropriate blessing" (Breisheet 49:28). Yaakov's blessing was a prophetic designation of each tribe's unique character, and what each tribe would contribute to the national enterprise. Accordingly, each tribe was matched, through Providence, with the region that most conformed to its nature and destiny, and would most benefit the nation as a whole. This is something that even Yehoshua could not determine unilaterally, because as a member of one particular tribe, even his motives would be suspected by some. The process had to be directed from Heaven, in order to complement each tribe with that part of *Eretz Yisrael* from which it would be able to extract its holiness.

The land of Israel is valued not for its commercial potential, but for its innate spiritual qualities – "a land that Hashem seeks out, the eyes of Hashem are always upon it, from the beginning of the year until year's end" (Devarim 11:12). Rav Tzvi Yehuda HaKohen Kook explained the verse "and I will provide (literally, feed) you the heritage of your father Yaakov" (Yeshayahu 58:14) to mean that the land of Israel nourishes the Jewish people and gives us life. The distribution of land was therefore not a mechanical act that required only map-drawing and settlement; it demanded physical conquest, followed by an "understanding" of the distinctiveness of each plot and parcel and its applicability to the tribal character. Hence, the division took a full seven years – and the names of the tribal regions are still used today – Yehuda, Binyamin, Menashe, Zevulun, etc. There is a special character that is stamped on the land itself and was also a reflection of its tribal owner. That is one reason why the Torah placed so much emphasis on ancestral land, its recovery by an owner forced to sell, and

---

24. Based on *Me'avoor Ha'aretz*, page 163.

its reversion to the original owner – under defined parameters – at the beginning of the Jubilee year.[25]

There are whole chapters in the Book of Yehoshua (13–21) that do little more than list place names, many of which are unfamiliar to us today. But these are not mere names; each name describes the quality of the place and the uniqueness of the tribe. We may not be able to deduce every concept to which the Navi is alluding, but assuredly it was a communication of great significance to the recipient who comprehended the message.[26] Millennia removed from this process, we can only grasp at the simplest correlation between tribe and territory (for example, Zevulun the seafarer was given Akko and the coast) but no more. That precious insight into the land of Israel has been lost for now, and our absolute and unchallenged possession of the land is therefore incomplete.

Similarly, we have a glimpse of the tribal character through the blessings of Yaakov, the type of stone that represented each tribe on the *kohen gadol*'s breastplate, the color and design on the tribal banner, and the identity of the tribal hero who reflected the tribal character in its most perfected form.[27] But even our knowledge of the tribal personality is somewhat incomplete, due to the length of the exile and our concomitant separation from the land of Israel and the world of the tribes. Full comprehension of the indissoluble link between the land of Israel, in whole and in part, and the Jewish people, as a nation and divided into tribes, still awaits the future redemption. When the land is fully revived and Jewish national life is rejuvenated according to the Torah, then we will appreciate – in detail – the integration of the people and the land. Then, as well, the inherent connection and indivisibility of the land and the people will be embraced by all Jews, and acknowledged by the international community.

The focus of the post-Yom Kippur War settlement movement was not exclusively a political or nationalistic act, as the hostile world and many Israelis perceived it, but an effort to once again revitalize the relationship between the people of Israel and the land of Israel so that the character of the land can make an impression on the people – and vice versa. By renam-

---

25. Vayikra 25:23–31; 27:16–24.
26. *Me'avoor Ha'aretz*, page 167. Rav Remer wrote that we are akin to people who can identify all the notes of a musical composition but do not know the melody.
27. Ibid. E.g., Shimshon (from the tribe of Dan), Gideon (from Menashe) or Ehud and Shaul (Binyamin).

ing these areas with their Biblical names[28] – and resettling these places with Torah-abiding Jews – the settlers attempt to bring to life the connection between the people and the land, and rebuild the foundation that Yehoshua laid through the original division of the land. That their efforts are unappreciated by many, and openly thwarted by some, reflects the spiritual distance yet to be traversed by the Chosen People and the "desirable, good and expansive land"[29] Hashem promised to our forefathers.

There were shortcomings in the division, as well. The apportionment of the land was not the direct word of Hashem, to which the people had become accustomed in the wilderness; it was carried out indirectly, through the *Urim v'Tumim* and the lottery. As grand as it was, it was still a diminution of their previous status. The division was also targeted and purposeful, and accounted for "problematic" features of certain tribes. For example, the tribe of Shimon, historically subversives and provocateurs, was banished to the south, without any neighbors except for the ruling tribe of Yehuda. (In due course – during the era of the *Shoftim* – Shimon's territory would be incorporated into Yehuda's land.[30]) Two and a half tribes did not receive any land in Israel, for they preferred to live in Transjordan. The forty-eight cities of the *Levi'im* were scattered throughout the land of Israel. All this indicated that the process was imperfect, as if a complete distribution of the land – as had been intended – was even now not possible, and would have to be postponed indefinitely.

This was the unfortunate legacy of the sin of the spies – "And they despised the desirable land, they had no faith in His word" (Tehillim 106:24) – that so diminished the connection between Hashem and the people, and the people and the land, that we have not yet recovered from it. The generation that entered the land was on a lower level than the generation that received the Torah, and sensed the attenuation of their relationship with Hashem. There was some discontent, even disappointment, in the nature of the distribution, and certainly the inability to fully conquer the land and drive out the inhabitants before the distribution lessened the people's enthusiasm for the process.

Indeed, the Jewish people did not long enjoy the apportionment of

---

28. Bet El, Eli, Shiloh, Maaleh Levona, Ofra, Atzmona, etc.
29. From the second blessing of Birkat HaMazon.
30. The tribe of Shimon became itinerant teachers.

the land according to these precise boundaries. Shortly, in the era of the *Shoftim* when anarchy reigned for long periods of time, the tribes would begin to intermarry, and these borders – and the demarcation of tribal character – would be diluted. The apex of Jewish life – fully-functioning tribes dwelling on their ancestral lands, worshipping the same God and observing the same Torah notwithstanding tribal diversity – was but a fleeting moment in the long span of Jewish history.

Yet, Jewish history is a continuum, and the land of Israel will again be apportioned in the Messianic era. All the flaws associated with the first division will be rectified. As the Gemara (Bava Batra 122a) states:

> The distribution of land in the world-to-come (i.e., the world of Moshiach) will not be like the distribution in this world. In this world, if a person has a wheat field, he does not have an orchard; if he has an orchard, he does not have a wheat field. In the world-to-come, every person will possess land in the mountains, the plains and the valleys…[31] In the world-to-come, Hashem Himself will divide the land among the people… In the world-to-come, the land will be allotted to thirteen tribes, with the additional portion awarded to the Moshiach.

There will be other changes as well, inferred from the book of Yechezkel (Chapter 48, the final chapter). In the Messianic era, the land will be divided amongst the tribes along a north-south axis. No tribe will live side-by-side with another. Dan will dwell in the northernmost part of expanded *Eretz Yisrael* (in what is today the Mediterranean coast of Syria), and Gad will dwell in the southernmost portion of *Eretz Yisrael*, in the Negev region. No Jew will live in Transjordan, so no division of land will take place there. Additionally, the cities of the *kohanim* and *Levi'im* will be clustered around Yerushalayim, and not dispersed throughout the country as in Yehoshua's time.

The future division of the land will rectify all the problems that plagued the original division. There will be a greater unity among the tribes, and the national servants (*kohanim* and *Levi'im*) will reside in the center of the land – accessible to all tribes and adjacent to Yerushalayim. Hashem will distribute the land, testifying to the renewed covenant, and as

---

31. I.e., there will be complete satisfaction with one's portion, and no person will have cause to begrudge the property of another.

a consequence of this divine intervention, every Jew will be content with his portion and rejoice in his friend's portion.

In the world of Moshiach, we will fully comprehend the dual aspects that constitute the Jewish intellectual essence: the ideas of God that are actualized in a national context. In an immature state, we tend to perceive our religious life as purely individual; in today's idiom, certain actions are private, "between man and God," in which there is no public interest. We fail to recognize that, for Jews, there is a pronounced national dimension in everything we do, public or private. There is no such thing as a private relationship with Hashem. Originally, we had a very sharp definition of roles; the *kohanim* and *Levi'im* were even a bit unworldly, removed from the mundane aspects of life and denied any inheritance in the land. The king of Israel was a glorified individual, "from the shoulder upward taller than anyone else,"[32] with an exalted personality – but who evoked either admiration or envy in the people, and was not always universally applauded or even worthy of the role.[33]

The shallowness of that perspective is exposed in the Messianic era. We will no longer be separated by our individuality but will acknowledge that we are all agents of one community. We are all musicians in one orchestra, but playing different instruments. We will all recognize that we each have a national role to play in the sanctification of Jewish life and of the land of Israel. We will acknowledge the power of the *tzibur* (community), and Hashem's vision of establishing not a confederation of disparate holy individuals but a "kingdom of priests and a holy nation" (Shemot 19:6). We will not live at loggerheads, with incompatible conceptions of Jewish life, and competing agendas that require fractious, unstable and transitory coalitions. That is a world with which we have grown too familiar – with politicians and political parties of ever-shifting values, principles and allegiances – and whose unpleasantness taints our national identity.

Every Jew is obligated to actualize the spiritual potential of *Eretz Yisrael*, and make the land itself bond with the people who have been endowed by the Creator with that very mandate – in order to glorify His name and perfect His world. The mission of the Jewish people – to carry Hashem's word and moral code to the nations – is based in *Eretz Yisrael*

---

32. The Navi's description of Shaul, cited from 1 Shmuel 10:23.
33. *Me'avoor Ha'aretz*, page 179.

and goes forth from *Eretz Yisrael*. Our history is a record of our attempts to execute that assignment, and our struggles against external foes and internal malfunctions. It is a history of stops and starts, and opportunities and failures followed by more opportunities and more failures, of glories and tragedies, and of exiles and homecomings.

The sin of the spies diminished our capacity to appreciate the land we were bequeathed, and Yehoshua's division of the land reflected this. It also subtly engendered the period of decline that began after the death of Yehoshua. The chaotic years of the *Shoftim* were characterized by divisiveness, civil wars, an absence of a strong, central leadership, and summarized in the closing words: "In those days there was no king in Israel; a man would do whatever seemed proper in his eyes" (Shoftim 21:25). The tribes in Transjordan would even build their own Tabernacle, so as not to be "burdened" with joining other Jews at the Tabernacle in Shiloh – and only backed down upon threat of civil war.

The conquest and settlement of the land of Israel was designed to complete the infrastructure of Jewish life, which would enable us to serve as Hashem's faithful representatives. It was intended to be the ultimate place of Jewish unity and stability. But man is given free choice, and *Eretz Yisrael* soon saw the fragmentation of the Jewish people into twelve separate tribes with twelve separate agendas. There was a loose association rather than a united nation, and we paid a terrible price with several centuries of strife interspersed with decades of tranquility.

Certainly the modern return to Zion is still incomplete, and not only because half the Jewish people still dwell in exile. There are renewed struggles over all the issues that Yehoshua tried to address: the equitable allocation of resources, the division of roles in Jewish life, the very nature of the Jewish mission, and even the question of whether there is any spiritual significance to the land of Israel and to our residence therein. There are growing doubts in certain sectors of the population as to whether the Jewish claim to the land of Israel is legitimate and/or exclusive. There is a prevalent fear of a complete rupture in Israeli society, with factions that have little common ground and competing national visions – perhaps twelve in all, like the ancient tribes. There is a hostile indigenous population whose future disposition defies any simple resolution, and a sufficient number of neighbors whose relentless antagonism requires constant vigilance. There are few leaders, if any, who can articulate the national, spiritual aspirations of the Jewish people in a manner in which they can resonate with any segment of the population beyond their own small circle of followers.

In addition, it can be argued that much of the world is ill-disposed towards Israel and not yet reconciled to the existence or even necessity of a Jewish national home. The world is preoccupied – even obsessed – with the resettlement of the land of Israel. It is literally true that thousands of people die of starvation or brutality while the world's leaders debate the propriety of building a few apartments in Maale Adumim, and this has become the norm in the diplomatic world.

These concerns are the growing pains of our reborn national life which was dormant for almost two thousand years. Overcoming these issues will necessitate an enhanced understanding of Jewish life, a deeper comprehension of Jewish destiny, and a focused commitment to the ideals of the Torah.

Rav Moshe Charlap, the great disciple and contemporary of Rav Avraham Yitzchak HaKohen Kook, once said (perhaps fifty years ago!) that the most important issue facing the Jewish people in any generation is that aspect of Jewish life that the nations of the world most vehemently oppose. The nations are the litmus test; whatever most agonizes them is clearly – to them – the greatest threat that the Jewish people pose to their worldview. Each era has its own passion. In other times, it was the antagonism towards circumcision, Shabbat, or other *mitzvot*; or the forced conversion of Jews; or even, in the Holocaust, the extermination of every Jew. In our generation, it is clear that the nations are fixated on the settlement of the land of Israel; nothing arouses as much fury in the corridors of power as the desire of a Jew living in Yitzhar or Hevron to build an extension to his home, or to move across the street to a new home.[34]

Clearly, then, the *mitzva* of *Yishuv Eretz Yisrael* (the settlement of the land of Israel) is the most pressing issue on the Jewish agenda. But it requires more than the physical settlement of land; it requires that the people of Israel remain spiritually connected to the land itself, and continue to extract its holiness and become energized by it. It requires immersion in the study of Torah, the fervent performance of *mitzvot*, and the pursuit of virtuous conduct. It requires a holistic life, in which all our endeavors – even those that are perceived as mundane and secular – are

---

34. *Torat Eretz Yisrael*, by Rabbi Samson, page 351.

consecrated. And then, symbiotically, sanctity will itself take root in the land, and in its people.

This was the goal of the first division of the land, which was not completely successful and therefore was not permanent. In the future, the apportionment of *Eretz Yisrael* will be permanent and the covenant with our forefathers will be fulfilled in its entirety. That will herald an era of peace and serenity, when "the earth will be filled with knowledge of Hashem as water covers the sea" (Yeshayahu 11:9).

Summary

The apportionment of the land of Israel was the purpose and culmination of the Book of Yehoshua, and laid the framework for the ideal Jewish existence as envisioned by the Torah. Its success was short-lived, due to our poor choices, and reinforced the lesson that mere settlement of the land is a transitory phenomenon unless such settlement is imbued with the rationale for Jewish national life: to be a holy people, created by God to declare His praise.[35] The land of Israel is not an end in itself but a means to an end – the headquarters of God's kingdom on earth.

---

35. Yeshayahu 43:21.

Epilogue

Yehoshua bid farewell to his people by reiterating the fundamental mandates of the Torah: to serve Hashem faithfully, observe the *mitzvot,* eschew idolatry and avoid entanglements with the indigenous population that still remained (Chapters 23–24). The people ratified the covenant again and pledged their loyalty. Yehoshua died with his mission not completely fulfilled. He had crossed the Jordan, apportioned the land, settled the people, established the Tabernacle at Gilgal, and laid the foundation for a Torah society – but the conquest was incomplete and the sublime promise made to our fathers would not be fully realized for almost four centuries.

To look, therefore, at Yehoshua's life as a failure or even just as a minimal success would be a grievous error, reflective of our own generation's stereotypical impatience. We are the "microwave generation." We want to take raw food and have it fully cooked and ready to eat in just several minutes. But good food, and the infrastructure of a Jewish state, require additional time, and building the Torah state – as we saw with Yehoshua – can require lifetimes and even centuries. Each generation builds on the achievements of the prior one, because each sees itself as part of a continuum of Jewish life.

This was Yehoshua's greatest strength and his prime qualification for the pivotal role he played in Jewish history. Whereas Moshe's insubordinate spies each had his own agenda, Yehoshua perceived his assignment as the fulfillment of the covenant with the *Avot*. He was the one entrusted to implement God's promises to Avraham, Yitzchak and Yaakov. Our Sages, as always, depicted this concept ingeniously. The Gemara (Sanhedrin 107a) states that the letter *yud*, taken from our mother Sarah's name,[1] "cried out in protest for years until [God] added it to Yehoshua's name."[2] In essence, the accomplishments of the *Avot* and *Imahot* (their "names") were unfinished until Yehoshua completed their mission. He led the Jewish people into the land, not only as the designee of Hashem but also as the agent of the *Avot*.[3]

For sure, there remains a profound difference in attitude and commitment today between those who see Jewish or Israeli history as a little more than a century old,[4] and those who view Jewish history as a continuum dating back to God's commandment to Avraham to "go forth from your land, from your relatives, and from your father's house to the land that I will show you" (Breisheet 12:1), consider the State of Israel as part of that grand dynamic, and literally walk in the footsteps of our forefathers throughout the length and breadth of the land. Those who feel an intense spiritual connection with the *Avot* have a perspective on events that is not shaped or dominated by temporal politics or diplomacy; it is a more natural, and more Jewish, connection.

The land of Israel demands not only physical conquest, but also the endowment of its soil with the sanctity of the Torah and its Jewish inhabitants. That can take time, as it depends solely on the *bechira*, the free choice, of its settlers and citizens. Centuries would elapse until the First Jewish Commonwealth was consolidated under the reign of David and Shlomo. This is surely sobering to those who have become irritated with the modern State of Israel's growing pains, and its inability to satisfy all of our hopes, dreams and expectations in the less than *six decades* of its existence.

1. The Torah (Breisheet 17:5 and 17:15) records that both Avraham and Sarah had their names changed by God. In Avraham's case, the letter *heh* was added to Avram, and the *yud* in Sarai was dropped and replaced by a *heh* as well. Note that in Jewish numerology, the two additional *heh*'s are the numerical equivalent of the one *yud*. That *yud* from Sarai "dangled" until it prefaced Yehoshua's name.
2. As the Torah indicates, Yehoshua was originally named Hoshea, until Moshe changed it on the eve of the spies' mission, in effect adding a *yud*: "And Moshe called Hoshea bin Nun *Yehoshua*" (Bamidbar 13:16). This was a prayer that God should save Yehoshua from the conspiracy of the spies (Rashi, ibid.).
3. Heard from my brother-in-law, Rabbi David Singer of Efrat, Israel.
4. As if Jewish history began with Theodor Herzl.

This impatience is a flaw in us, for sure, but its converse should nonetheless not be utilized to rationalize failures or mistakes, or the occasional attempt to flee from the realities of Jewish destiny.

Jewish history is an inexorable march to redemption. Usually we march forward, but intermittently there are reverses as well. Some unfortunate moves set us back decades or centuries, but the end of the process is known to us through the words of our prophets. We have tasted success – military triumphs, the settlement of the land, the extension of Jewish sovereignty throughout the land of Israel, the proliferation of Torah ideals – and obstacles, as well, which have left the conquest only partially finished. And this refers both to Yehoshua's time and to our time.

Yehoshua, the devoted disciple of Moshe and the great conqueror of the land of Israel, died at the age of 110 and was buried in Timnat-Serach (Yehoshua 24:29–30),[5] a short distance from the modern city of Ariel in the mountains of Efraim. Today, the gravesite of the conqueror of Israel is under Arab control, and pilgrimages by Jews are infrequent, arduous and dangerous. It is a reminder to us that the destiny of Israel is influenced by our deeds but controlled by Hashem, and will yet unfold as Hashem ordains, in its time and in all its majesty.

---

5. This same place is called Timnat-Cheres in Shoftim 2:9.

About the Author

RABBI STEVEN PRUZANSKY is the spiritual leader of Congregation Bnai Yeshurun, in Teaneck, New Jersey, one of the most vibrant centers of Orthodox Jewish life today, and currently serves as the President of the Rabbinical Council of Bergen County. Previously, Rabbi Pruzansky was for nine years the spiritual leader of Congregation Etz Chaim in Kew Gardens Hills, New York. While in New York, he served a two-year term as President of the Vaad Harabonim (Rabbinical Board) of Queens.

Rabbi Pruzansky graduated from Columbia University in 1978 with a B.A. in history, and received a Juris Doctor degree from the Benjamin Cardozo School of Law in 1981. He practiced law for 13 years as a general practitioner and litigator in New York City until assuming his current pulpit. Rabbi Pruzansky studied in yeshivot in Israel and the United States, and was ordained at Yeshiva Bnei Torah of Far Rockaway, New York under the guidance of Rabbi Yisrael Chait, shlit"a.

He currently serves as President of the Rabbinical Board of Bergen County, in addition to being a member of the Executive Committee of the Rabbinical Council of America. Active in a host of Jewish organizations, Rabbi Pruzansky has also received numerous awards, especially for his advocacy on behalf of the State of Israel and the Jewish people.

Rabbi Pruzansky is widely-sought as a lecturer and writer on topics of Jewish interest.